ARCHITECTURE
SOURCEBOOK

ARCHITECTURE SOURCEBOOK

Russell Sturgis

VNR VAN NOSTRAND REINHOLD COMPANY

Library of Congress Catalog Card Number 84-7275
ISBN 0-442-28031-9

Printed in the United States of America

Published by Van Nostrand Reinhold Company Inc.
135 West 50th Street
New York, New York 10020

Van Nostrand Reinhold Company Limited
Molly Millars Lane
Wokingham, Berkshire RG11 2PY, England

Van Nostrand Reinhold
480 La Trobe Street
Melbourne, Victoria 3000, Australia

Macmillan of Canada
Division of Gage Publishing Limited
164 Commander Boulevard
Agincourt, Ontario M1S 3C7, Canada

16 15 14 13 12 11 10 9 8 7 6 5 4 3 2 1

Library of Congress Cataloging in Publication Data

Sturgis, Russell.
   Architecture sourcebook.

   1. Architecture—Details.   2. Decoration and ornament, Architectural. I. Title.
   NA2840.S78   1984   720′.22′2   84-7275
   ISBN 0-442-28031-9

ARCHITECTURE SOURCEBOOK

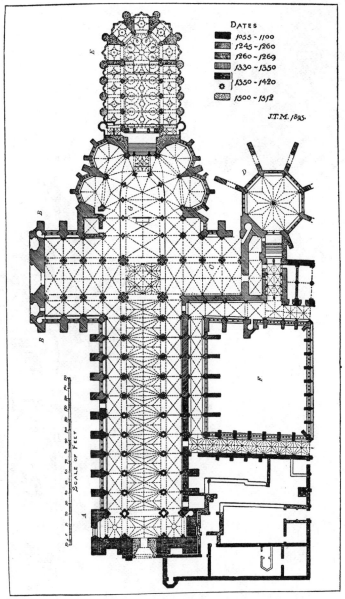

WESTMINSTER ABBEY, LONDON.

A. Nave, of which the eastern part is used as the choir. *B*. North transept; the three bays of the eastern aisle are used as chapels. *C*. South transept, of which the western aisle is thrown into the cloister: the remainder is the "Poets' Corner." *D*. Chapter house. *E*. Henry the Seventh's Chapel. *F*. Cloister. *G*. Edward the Confessor's Chapel.

ACANTHUS.
As modified in Roman work.

ACANTHUS, NATURAL.
From drawing by John Ruskin.

ACANTHUS, NATURAL.
From drawing by John Ruskin.

OPEN

ACCOLADE.

A three-centred arch with reversed curve and finial. French work, 15th century.

ACCOUPLEMENT OF ENGAGED COLUMNS; HÔTEL D'ASSEZAT,
TOULOUSE, FRANCE.

ACCOUPLEMENT OF PILASTERS; CHURCH OF S. GIORGIO MAGGIORE, VENICE.

A PLAN OF THE ACROPOLIS OF ATHENS.

5. Temple of Nike Apteros.
6. Propylæa.
12. Fortified wall of Pelasgic work.
13. Precinct of Artemis Brauronia.
20. ⎱ The two modern museums.
21. ⎰
22. Parthenon.
26. Roman Temple (traces only).
31. Erechtheum.
34. Temple of Athena before the Persian invasion.
40. Place of colossal bronze statue of Athena Promachos.
42. Theatre of Dionysus.
45. Choragic Monument of Thrasyllus.
47. Sanctuary of Æsculapius.
51. Portico of Eumenes.
52. Odeum of Herodes Atticus.

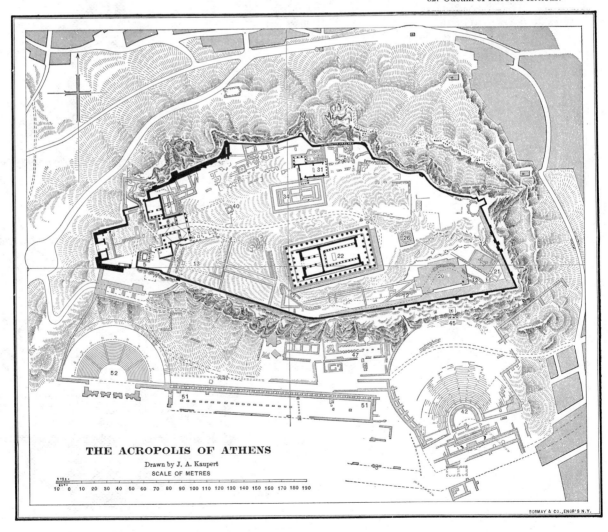

THE ACROPOLIS OF ATHENS

Drawn by J. A. Kaupert
SCALE OF METRES

10 0 10 20 30 40 50 60 70 80 90 100 110 120 130 140 150 160 170 180 190

AISLE: SOUTH AISLE OF PETERBOROUGH CATHEDRAL.

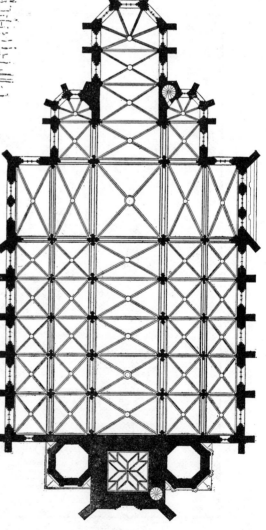

AISLED: A FIVE-AISLED CHURCH; CHURCH OF S. MARY,
MULHAUSEN, PRUSSIA, GERMANY.

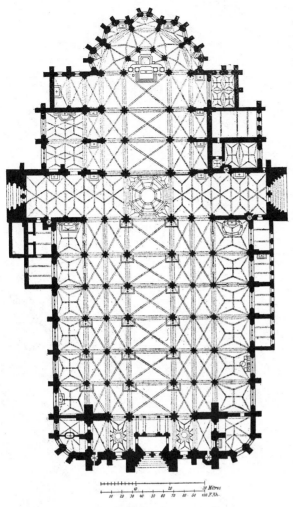

AISLED: A SEVEN-AISLED CHURCH; THE CATHEDRAL OF
ANTWERP, BELGIUM.

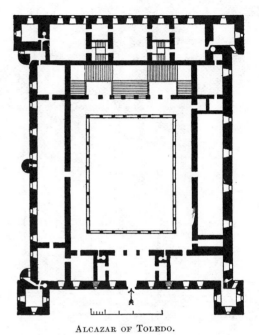

ALCAZAR OF TOLEDO.

Plan at level of great Patio, which is a noble court with double
arcade.   The exterior is like that of a fortress

11

ALETTE: THE WING OF THE PIER ON EITHER SIDE OF EACH
ENGAGED COLUMN.

Restoration by Viollet-le-Duc of the Order of the Theatre of Marcellus at Rome.
The Doric columns of the lower story are now known to have a base.

THE ALHAMBRA, GRANADA, SPAIN.
Construction of the arcading, Court of the Lions.

ALHAMBRA FROM THE SOUTHWEST.

ALLÈGE.
From a 5th-century building in Syria.

ALTAR: GRECO-ROMAN WORK.

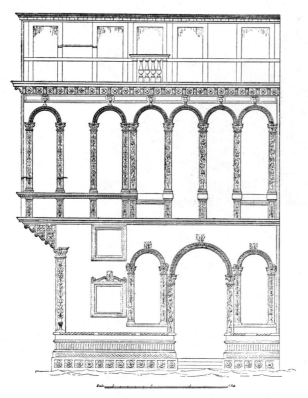

ALLEY: FRONT OF A HOUSE OF THE CLOSE OF THE 15TH
CENTURY ON RIO DI FAVA, VENICE.

The overhang on the left is above a narrow alley which leads to water steps.

ALTAR WITH CANOPY; RATISBON CATHEDRAL.

ALTAR: WENLOCK PRIORY, SHROPSHIRE, c. 1450.

14

ALTAR: S. ANTONIO AT PADUA; ITALIAN WORK, LATE 14TH CENTURY.

ALTAR OF THE MOST HOLY SACRAMENT; CHURCH OF SS.
GERVASIO E PROTASIO.

The whole is sculptured in marble; the effect of perspective in the middle being
produced by shallow relief and intaglio.

ALTAR RAIL FROM S. M. DEI MIRACOLI, VENICE.

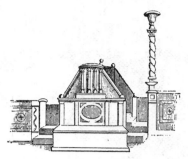

AMBO: GOSPEL SIDE; CHURCH OF S. CLEMENT, ROME.

AMBO: EPISTLE SIDE; CHURCH (BASILICA) OF S. CLEMENT, ROME.

AMBRY: 14TH CENTURY: CHURCH OF FOULIS, PERTHSHIRE, SCOTLAND.

AMBULATORY OF THE CLOISTER; ABBEY OF ROMMERSDORF, NEAR NEUWIED, GERMANY.

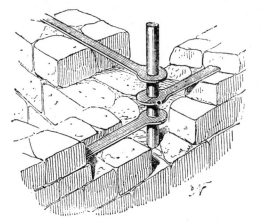

ANCHOR WITHOUT ORNAMENTAL HEAD, TO SECURE
CROSS WALL OR PARTITION TO EXTERIOR WALL,
THREE STEEL RIBBONS WITH FIXED PIN.

ANCHOR: 14TH CENTURY; WROUGHT-IRON FLEUR-
DE-LIS FOR HEAD.

FOUR ANCHORS, THE HEADS GIVING THE DATE
"1584."

ANCHOR WITH HEAD, GIVING CIPHER, "C. R."

ANCONA.

ANGLE SHAFT: CURIOUS GROUP OF TWO SHAFTS;
FRENCH, 13TH CENTURY.

ANGLE SHAFT: VENICE, 14TH CENTURY.

The term may be applied as well to the free, supporting
column, as to the engaged shaft above.

ANNULATED COL-
UMN FROM WHIT-
BY   ABBEY,
YORKSHIRE.

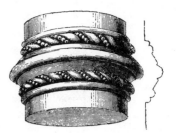

ANNULATED COLUMN FROM
CHURCH OF S. PETER, NORTH-
AMPTON.

ANNULETS AT NECKING OF GRECIAN DORIC CAPITAL.

ANTHEMIONS CARVED UPON THE CYMATIUM OF THE RAKING
CORNICE ABOVE THE PEDIMENT OF A TEMPLE.

There are three patterns, combining to form an anthemion moulding of unusual richness.

IN ANTIS: SYRIAN PORTICO; 4TH OR 5TH CENTURY A.D.

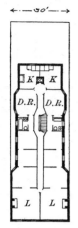

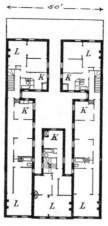

APARTMENT HOUSE:
FIG. 1. TWO APART-
MENTS TO A FLOOR.

A house with apartments
of this character is
more often called Ten-
ement House (which
see). In this and the
other figures, *L.* Liv-
ing Room (often called
Parlour), *K.* Kitchen,
P. Parlour, *D. R.* Dining Room.

APARTMENT
HOUSE:
FIG. 2.

APARTMENT HOUSE:
FIG. 3.

APARTMENT HOUSE:
FIG. 4.

The room *B* may be a
library or boudoir.

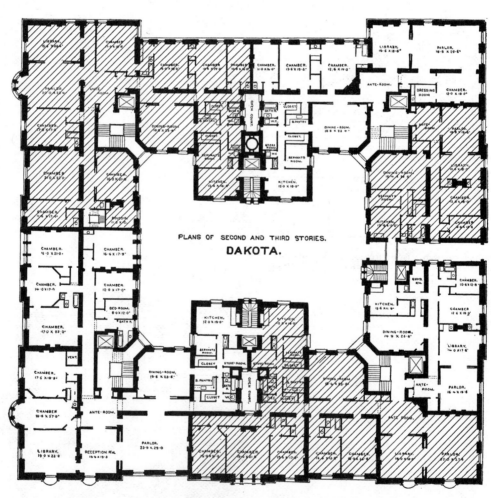

PLANS OF SECOND AND THIRD STORIES.
DAKOTA.

APARTMENT HOUSE: "THE DAKOTA," NEW YORK: FIG. 5. (ARCHITECT, H. J. HARDENBERGH.)

Plan of an upper story, showing six separate dwellings.

APSE: SCOTTISH ROMANESQUE; DALMENY, LINLITHGOWSHIRE, C. 1150.

APSE: ENGLISH ROMANESQUE; ROMSEY, HANTS,
c. 1180.

APSE: ENGLISH, 13TH CENTURY; TIDMARSH, BERKSHIRE.

21

APSE: S. GEORGIO AL VELABRO, ROME.

APSE: SPANISH ROMANESQUE, 12TH CENTURY.

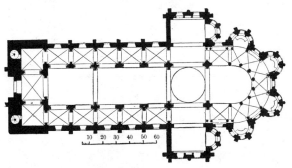

APSE CHAPEL, CHURCH OF NOTRE-DAME-DU-PORT, CLERMONT-
FERRAND.

With four apse chapels and two apses (or apsidioles) at east side of transept.

ARABESQUE: SPANISH, 16TH CENTURY.

ARABESQUE: SPANISH, 16TH CENTURY.

ARABESQUES IN CARVED WOOD.
Adorning a 15th century house at Rouen.

ARABESQUE, ELIZABETHAN.

ARABESQUE: EARLY 16TH CENTURY, ITALIAN TERRA COTTA.

ARCADE OF DECORATIVE PURPOSE; CHURCH OF
COLESHILL, WARWICKSHIRE.

ARCADE: SOUTH AISLE OF CHOIR, LINCOLN CATHEDRAL; 14TH CENTURY.

ARCADE: 15TH CENTURY; LINCOLN CATHEDRAL.

INTERSECTING ARCADE: CHRIST CHURCH, OXFORD;
CLOSE OF 12TH CENTURY.

ARCADE ON COURT, HÔTEL D'ASSEZAT, TOULOUSE; 16TH
CENTURY.

SURFACE ARCADE, STONE CHURCH, KENT.

NAVE ARCADE, BARTON STACEY, WILTSHIRE.

NAVE ARCADE, LINCOLN CATHEDRAL; EARLY 13TH CENTURY.

NAVE ARCADE, GREAT MALVERN CHURCH, WORCESTERSHIRE; 12TH CENTURY.

27

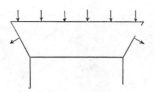

ARCH, FIG. 1.
The vertical pressure resolved into
two diagonal sideway pressures.

PRIMITIVE ARCH

TWO FLAT ARCHES

SEGMENTAL ARCH

THREE ROUND ARCHES

ROLLOCK ARCH

STILTED ARCH

TWO CUSPED ARCHES

BLUNT

EQUILATERAL

ACUTE OR LANCET

THREE POINTED ARCHES

THREE-CENTRED OR BASKET HANDLE ARCH

FOUR-CENTRED ARCH
WITH REVERSED CURVE AT POINT

TWO ITALIAN MODIFICATIONS OF THE POINTED ARCH

ARCH, FIG. 2.
Arches of different kinds shown as if all built in the same wall.

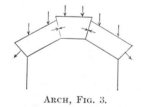

ARCH, FIG. 3.
The vertical pressures resolved into diagonal
sideway pressures at the two abutments,
and into reciprocal sideway pressures at
the two joints between the stones.

BELL ARCH.
From a belfry in a Swiss village above Vevay.

CHANCEL ARCH, HEADINGTON, OXFORDSHIRE;
MIDDLE 12TH CENTURY.

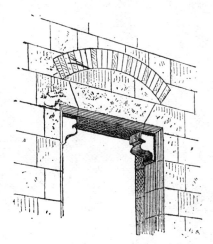

DISCHARGING ARCH OVER A FLAT ARCH, FORMING
LINTEL.

DISCHARGING ARCH OVER A WOODEN LINTEL.

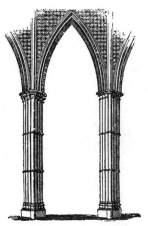

LANCET ARCH, WESTMINSTER
ABBEY.

ARCH: TRANSVERSE ARCH.

South aisle of the abbey church, Vézelay; transverse arch dividing the
compartments or vaulting squares.

ARCHITRAVE.

A 6th-century building in Syria, with architraves enclosing the square windows, and a bent
or broken architrave carried around the arch of the great doorway.

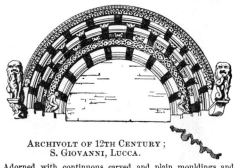

ARCHIVOLT OF 12TH CENTURY;
S. GIOVANNI, LUCCA.

Adorned with continuous carved and plain mouldings and
voussoirs carved and of contrasted colours.

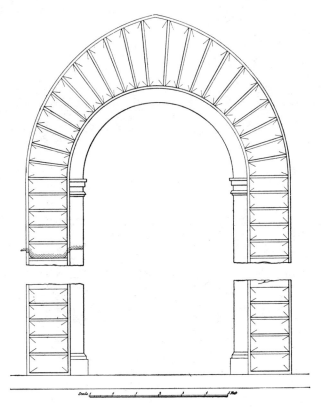

ARCHIVOLT: PALAZZO NICCOLINI, FLORENCE; 15TH CENTURY.
Each voussoir cut with rustication.

ARCHIVOLT: PALAZZO PAZZI-QUARATESI, FLORENCE;
15TH CENTURY.

ARMS PAINTED IN THE MINSTER, AACHEN
(AIX LA CHAPELLE).

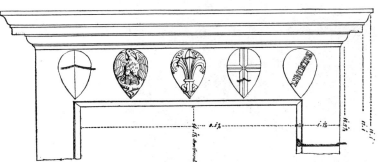

ARMS OF THE CITY (THE GIGLIO) AND OTHERS CARVED ON A LINTEL;
FLORENCE, ITALY.

ARMS, ROYAL, OF SWEDEN, VASA FAMILY, 1562;
CASTLE OF KALMAR.

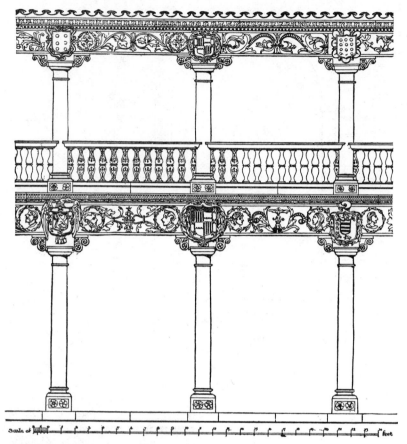

ARMS: HERALDIC BEARINGS ADORNING THE PATIO OF THE CASA POLENTINA, AVILA, SPAIN.

ASIA MINOR: STONE-CARVED TOMB FROM HOÏRAN.

ASIA MINOR: PEASANT'S HUT AT GYOBEN.

ASIA MINOR: MODERN LYCIAN GRANARY.

ATTIC: ARCH OF TRAJAN, BENEVENTO.
Having a very lofty attic bearing inscriptions and two bas-reliefs.

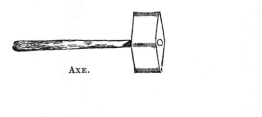

AXE.

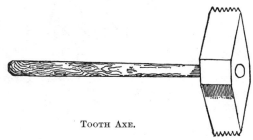

TOOTH AXE.

BALCONY: ISTRIAN STONE, 14TH CENTURY, WITH
SHAFTED BALUSTERS, AND HANDRAIL CUT TO
THE SEMBLANCE OF AN ARCADE; VENICE.

BALDACHIN OF S. PETER'S CHURCH (S. PIETRO IN VATICANO), ROME.
Designed by Bernini; of bronze; about 95 feet high (see cut of apse, S. Giorgio,
Al Velabro.)

BALL FLOWERS FROM KINGSTHORPE CHURCH,
NORTHAMPTONSHIRE; LATE 13TH CENTURY.

BALL FLOWERS: WINDOW TRACERY OF GLOUCES-
TER CATHEDRAL, 14TH CENTURY.

BALUSTER COLUMN
FROM S. ALBAN'S
CATHEDRAL; 11TH
OR 12TH CENTURY.

BALUSTRADE, FORMING ALLÈGE, ITS HAND RAIL FORMING THE SILL; FROM A
WINDOW IN THE COUR DE CASSATION, PARIS.

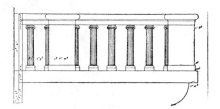

BALUSTRADE ORDER, FORMING THE PARAPET OF
THE PALAZZO PITTI, FLORENCE.

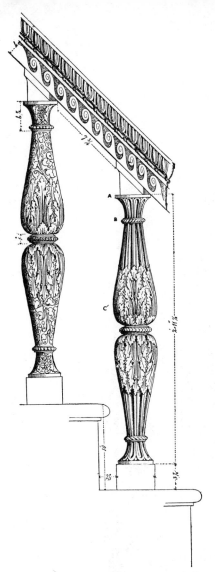

BALUSTER FROM THE PULPIT STAIRCASE, SIENA
CATHEDRAL.

The stair is of 1543, much later than the pulpit.

Coupe AB

BALUSTRADE OF STAIRS FROM A HOUSE IN THE
RUE DE LISBONNE, PARIS; WORK OF THE 19TH
CENTURY.

35

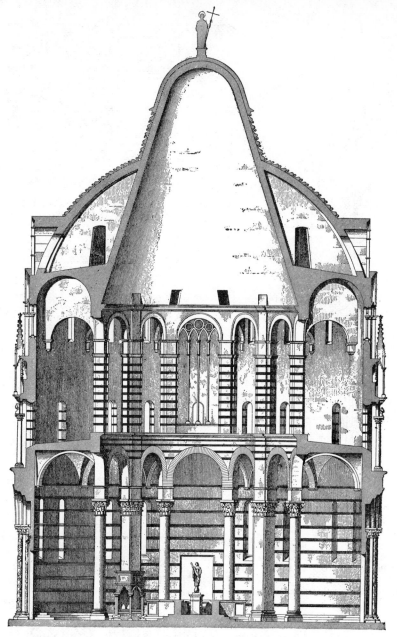

BAPTISTERY AT PISA: A ROUND CHURCH OF THE 12TH CENTURY.

This vertical section shows a conical roof over the central part, which corresponds to the nave of an oblong church, and vaulted aisles two stories high.   The curved outer cupola is a much later addition.

BAR OF AN OUTER DOOR; OLD HOUSE IN CHELSEA, MASS.

Bar: Temple Bar; London, 1670. Designed by Sir Christopher Wren.

Bargeboard at Shrewsbury, Shropshire; about 1350 (the Window is Later).

Bargeboard: Late 14th Century: Wingham, Kent, England.

BARN: STONE BARN OF THE MONASTERY, PILTON, SOMERSETSHIRE.

BAROCCO (GERMAN, BAROCK) ARCHITECTURE: STREET FRONT IN MUNICH; ABOUT 1760.

38

BAROCCO ARCHITECTURE: DOORWAY OF CHURCH
ON THE ESTATE OF TYRESÖ, SWEDEN.

BAROCCO ARCHITECTURE: DOORWAY OF A COURT
IN ANTWERP, BELGIUM; ABOUT 1663.

The other illustrations have shown more graceful types, this
shows an ugly and distorted one, of this widely prevalent
style of design.

BASE OF EGYPTIAN COL-
UMN IN THE RUINS OF
THEBES.

BASE OF IONIC ORDER; THE
ERECHTHEUM, ATHENS.

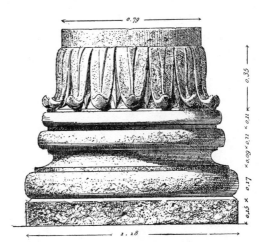

BASE OF LATE GREEK WORK IN SYRIA; TEMPLE
AT SOUEIDEH.

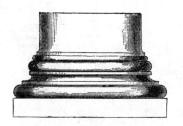

BASE OF IMPERIAL ROMAN STYLE FROM THE AQUEDUCT OF HADRIAN.

Compare with cut, Attic Base.

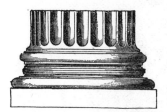

BASE OF CORINTHIAN ORDER FROM THE TEMPLE OF CASTOR, ROME.

ATTIC BASE: BASE OF CORINTHIAN ORDER, OF THE PATTERN PRESCRIBED BY VITRUVIUS, AND CALLED BY HIM ATTIC BASE.

BASE OF A WALL PIER, OR ENGAGED COLUMN; HADDISCOE CHURCH, NORFOLKSHIRE.

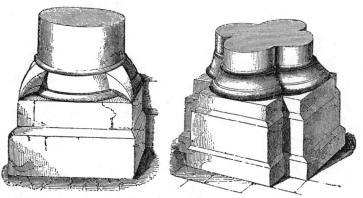

BASES AT S. PETER'S, NORTHAMPTONSHIRE; LATE 12TH CENTURY.

Base with spurs or griffes of a round column; Base of a clustered pier of quatrefoil section.

BASE OF CLUSTERED PIER WITH RICH SCULPTURE (AN UNUSUAL DECORATION): CHAPTER HOUSE, LINCOLN CATHEDRAL; ABOUT 1200.

BASE OF CLUSTERED PIER, SALISBURY
CATHEDRAL; ABOUT 1230.

BASE FROM BERNINI'S COLONNADE, PIAZZA DI SAN PIETRO, ROME; A.D. 1667.

BASEMENT, INCLUDING TWO STORIES, OF THE BUILDING PALAZZO GRASSI AT VENICE,
1705 A.D.

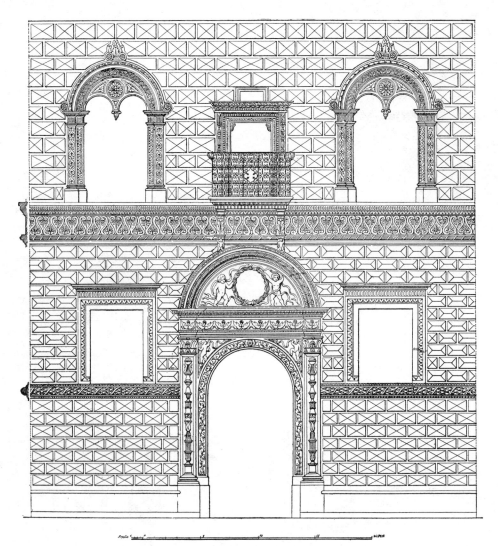

BASEMENT: PALAZZO BEVILACQUA, BOLOGNA.

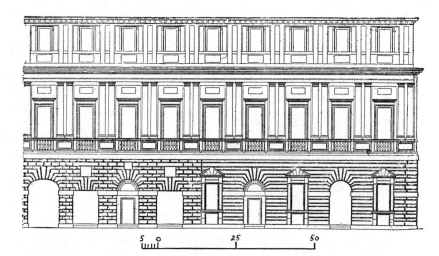

5 0   25   50

BASEMENT AS HIGH AS THE PRINCIPAL STORY — ABOUT 23 FEET: PALAZZO STOPPANI, ROME, 1515–1520 A.D.

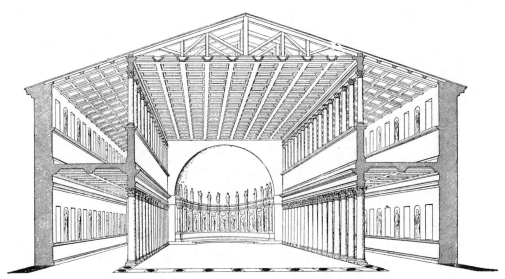

BASILICA: RESTORATION BY PALLADIO OF A TYPICAL ROMAN BASILICA.

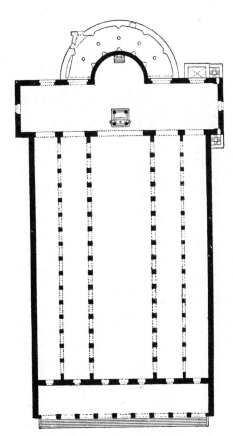

BASILICA OF S. JOHN LATERAN AT ROME, AS BUILT
IN THE 5TH CENTURY A.D.

Width within the outer walls, 180 feet.

BASILICA OF S. LORENZO WITHOUT THE WALLS. IN PART OF THE 4TH CENTURY A.D., MADE UP OF
FRAGMENTS OF IMPERIAL WORK.

BASILICA OF S. CLEMENTE, ROME; REBUILT IN THE 11TH CENTURY ON THE OLD PLAN.

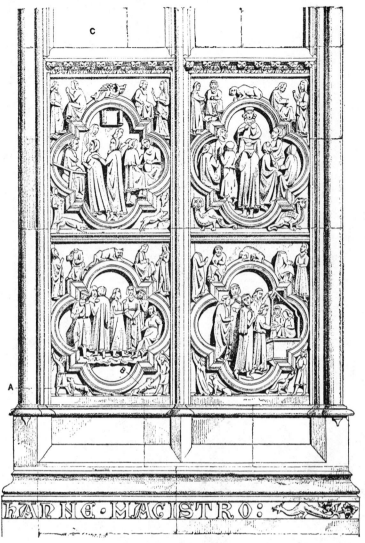

BAS-RELIEF OF THE 13TH CENTURY; NOTRE-DAME, PARIS. FOUR PANELS FROM A BUTTRESS OF SOUTH TRANSEPT.

BASTIDE: VIEW OF THE PUBLIC SQUARE AND COVERED STREET ADJOINING, AT MONPAZIER (DORDOGNE), SOUTHWESTERN FRANCE.

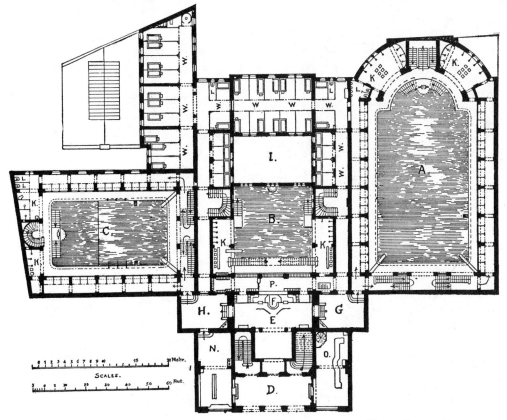

BATH HOUSE: NEW MUNICIPAL BATH HOUSE AT FRANKFORT-ON-THE-MAIN; GROUND FLOOR.

A. Swimming bath, first-class, for men.
B. Swimming bath, second-class, for men.
C. Swimming bath for women.
D. Open vestibule.
E. Inner vestibule.

F. Ticket office.
G. Waiting room for men.
H. Waiting room for women.
I. Inner court (open).
K. Cleansing and preliminary baths.

L. Water-closets.
N. Barber shop.
O. Restaurant.
P. Towels, etc.
W. Tub baths.

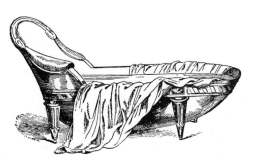

BATH TUB: "SOFA" BATH, 18TH CENTURY.

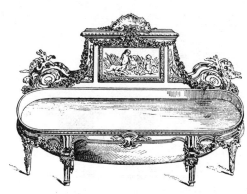

BATH TUB: "SOFA" BATH, 18TH CENTURY.

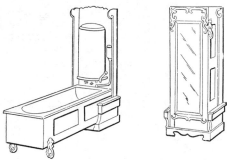

BATH TUB: STATIONARY FOLDING "CABINET"
BATH TUB, WITH WATER CISTERN WHICH CAN
BE CONNECTED WITH HEATER.

47

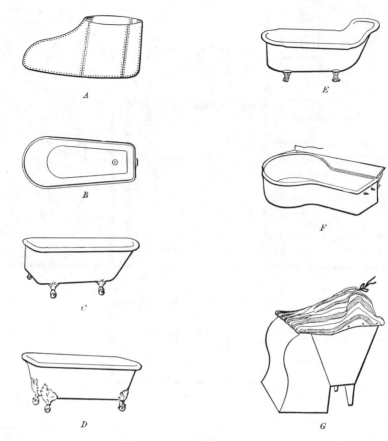

BATH TUBS OF DIFFERENT FORMS:

A. Slipper bath, ancient form.
B. Old pattern, tapering horizontally and vertically.
C. Recent " French " pattern, parallel sides.
D. " Roman " pattern.
E. Special form with head rest.
F. Special form, south of Europe.
G. Chair for vapour baths, with cover of rubber cloth.

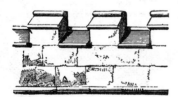

BATTLEMENTS OF DECORATIVE PURPOSE ; S. MARY'S CHURCH, BEVERLY, YORKSHIRE.

These are much smaller than the military battlements, and have mouldings and drips which are not used in the latter.

BATTLEMENT OF BRICK, OF DECORATIVE PURPOSE ; VERONA.

This is the pattern known as the Scaliger or La Scala Battlement.

BATTLEMENT FROM THE GAR-
DEN WALL OF A HOUSE IN
THE CALLE DEL BAGATIN,
VENICE.

BATTLEMENT OF BRICK FROM A GARDEN WALL;
VENICE.

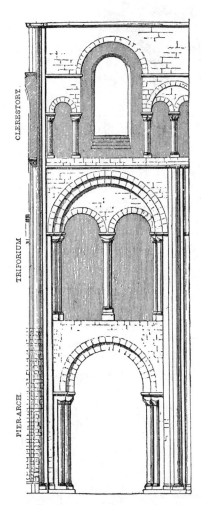

BAY OF TRANSEPT; WINCHESTER CATHEDRAL,
c. 1090.

The wall of the nave arcade, the triforium, and clerestory are
shown white; the more distant wall behind the triforium
and upper gallery is shaded. A series of such vertical com-
binations of three parts makes up the design of the interior.

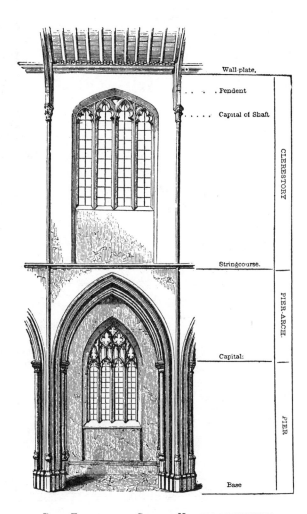

BAY: FOTHERINGAY CHURCH, NORTHAMPTONSHIRE,
c. 1440.

One of the units of design of the interior of a small church in
the perpendicular style, with a simple wooden roof. The
aisle is seen beyond the pillars of the nave arcade.

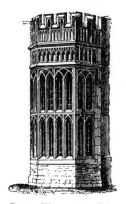

BAY WINDOW: PER-
PENDICULAR GOTHIC;
COMPTON CHURCH,
WINGATE, WAR-
WICKSHIRE.

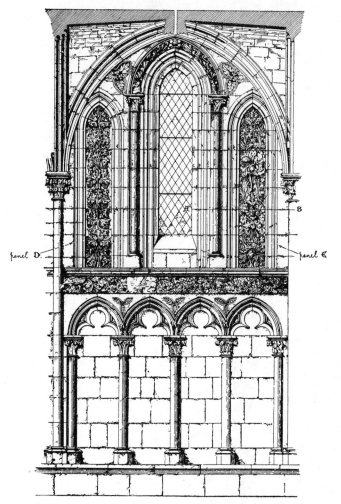

BAY OF THE OUTER WALL OF CHOIR AISLE; CHURCH
AT NORREY, NEAR CAEN.

An interesting wall arcade below, and very unusual panels filled with
carving above. Norman work, 14th century.

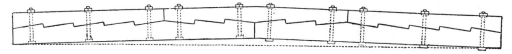

BUILT BEAM.

This beam is formed by uniting five pieces of timber by scarfs and bolts. The beam is formed with a slight camber to avoid
sagging. See illustration of Truss Beam.

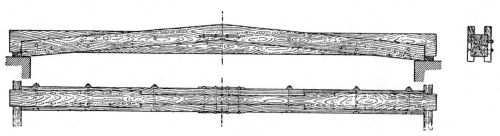

TRUSSED BEAM.

The beam (in the centre) is stiffened by two pairs of struts, secured on either side by scarfing and by bolts; the beam itself acting
as a tie. The whole acts as a simple truss and is a common form of Built Beam.

50

BED PLACES: PERMANENT; IN RICH PEASANT'S HOUSE, MODERN FRANCE.

BEFFROI: MONS, BELGIUM.

BELFRY OF CHURCH OF S. CHARLES BORROMEO AT
ANTWERP, C. 1620 A.D.

BELFRY OF THE CATHOLIC COURT CHURCH (HOF-
KIRCHE) AT DRESDEN.

BELFRY: INTERIOR OF WEST TOWER OF CHURCH AT
BERNIÈRES, NEAR CAEN (CALVADOS).

The bell ropes pass through holes in the vaulting to the church floor.

BELGIUM: CATHEDRAL OF TOURNAY. VIEW OF SOUTH TRANSEPT.

BELGIUM: CHURCH OF S. MICHEL, LOUVAIN, BELGIUM,
1650–1660 A.D.

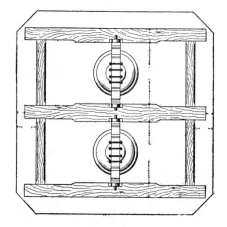

BELL CAGE: CHURCH OF S. JEAN BAPTISTE DE BELLEVILLE.

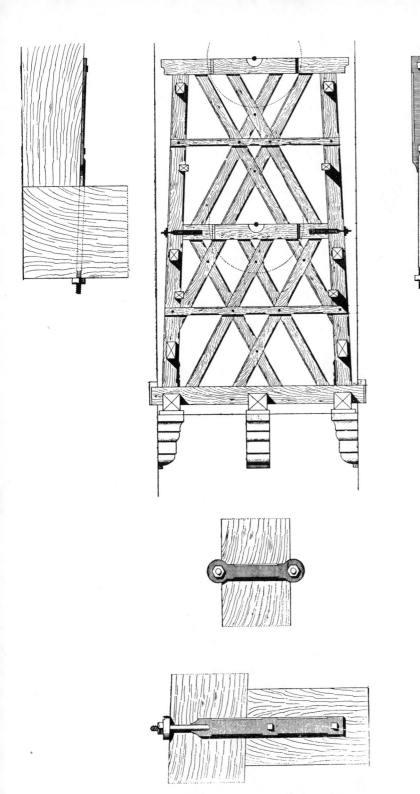

BELL CAGE: CHURCH OF S. JEAN BAPTISTE DE BELLEVILLE.

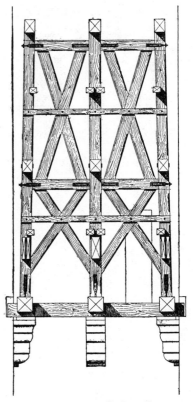

BELL CAGE: CHURCH OF S. JEAN BAPTISTE DE
BELLEVILLE.

BELL COTE: LITTLE COXWELL,
BERKSHIRE, C. 1200.

BELL GABLE: CHURCH OF LITTLE CASTERTON,
RUTLAND.

BELL COTE AT MITTOIS, NEAR CAEN (CALVADOS).
The light 13th century gable has been stayed by added masonry
which is covered and roofed with tiles.

BELL TOWER OF THE SIMPLEST FORM; CHURCH AT
TIERCEVILLE, NEAR CAEN (CALVADOS), FRANCE.

The tower has a saddle-back roof.

BELL TOWER OF OLD CATHEDRAL AT ZARAGOZA,
SPAIN, C. 1685 A.D.

BELL TURRET AT HARESCOMB, GLOUCESTERSHIRE.

BÉNITIER: CHURCH OF S. MARK,
VENICE. EARLY CINQUECEN-
TO WORK.

THE BIGALLO, OR LOGGIA DEL BIGALLO, FLORENCE.

BILLET MOULDING AT BINHAM
PRIORY, NORFOLKSHIRE.

BISHOP'S CHAIR IN CATHEDRAL AT AQUILEJA.

BLOCK HOUSE NEAR KUERDSCHEKOÏ, ASIA MINOR.

Described by Petersen and v. Luschan as very carefully built
of squared timbers and planks, showing, at the corners, the
interlocking construction characteristic of Lycia. The
building is raised on a mound of earth.

BOHEMIA: TEYNKIRCHE AT PRAGUE, 15TH CEN-
TURY. THE WEST FRONT.

BOHEMIA: KARLSBRÜCKE AT PRAGUE. WEST END WITH TOWERS.

BOHEMIA: TOWER AT PRAGUE IN THE ROSSMARKT.

BOLSTER IN SWISS WOODWORK, 18TH CENTURY.

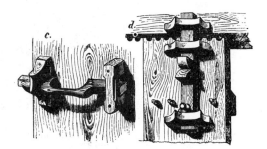

BOLT: WITH RINGS AND DOOR-PULL, ALL OF WOOD,
SWISS, 17TH CENTURY.

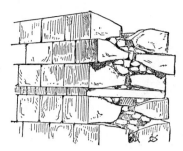

BOND AS USED IN EARLY STONE WORK OF SYRIA.

The thin course of headers are through stones and form a heart bond with the stones, above and below, which meet at the centre of the wall. These also form running bonds as shown at the face of the wall.

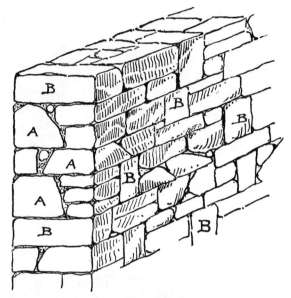

BOND AS FORMED IN A WALL OF ROUGH STONE; *B*, *B* BEING THROUGH STONES, AND *A*, *A* WHAT ARE SOMETIMES CALLED "THREE-QUARTER" BOND STONES. (SEE HEART BOND.)

BOND FORMED AT THE JUNCTION OF A CROSS WALL WITH AN OUTER WALL, THE BOND STONES BEING DRESSED TO THE EXACT THICKNESS OF THE WALLS, SO THAT THESE STRETCHERS SERVE ALSO AS PERPENDS.

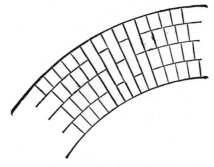

BLOCK IN COURSE BOND, FORMED BY FIVE COURSES
OF BONDED BRICK TO TIE TOGETHER THE FOUR
CONCENTRIC RINGS OF ROWLOCKS.

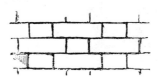

CLIP BOND, FORMED AT THE JUNCTION OF THE
DIAGONAL HEADERS AND THE FACE BRICKS
WHICH HAVE THEIR CORNERS "CLIPPED."

These headers also form a diagonal bond. (See illustration of
Plumb Bond.)

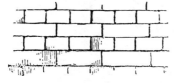

ENGLISH BOND.

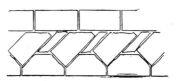

FLEMISH BOND.

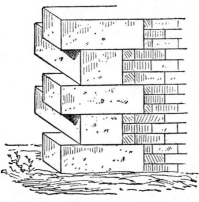

IN-AND-OUT BOND, FORMED BY A VERTICAL SERIES
OF CUT STONES INSERTED IN A BRICK WALL.

Here the headers are arranged to be incorporated in a cross-
wall, which will thus be bonded to the wall shown.

PLUMB BOND: THE RESULT OF BONDING THE FACE
BRICK AS SHOWN IN THE ILLUSTRATION OF
CLIP BOND.

The term is, however, used to describe the entire method, and
hence, commonly, as synonymous with Diagonal Bond.

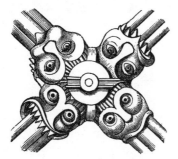

BOSS: CHURCH OF ELKSTONE, GLOUCESTERSHIRE.

BOSS: CHAPTER HOUSE, OXFORD CATHEDRAL, c. 1250.

BOSS: ST. ALBAN'S ABBEY CHURCH, HERTFORD-SHIRE.

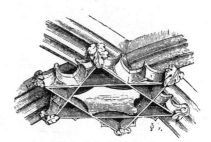

BOSS: CHURCH OF NOTRE-DAME LA RICHE, TOURS, 15TH CENTURY.

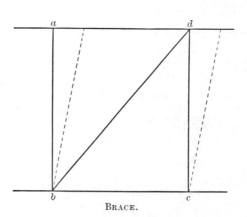

BRACE.

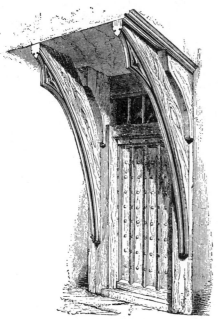

BRACKETS CARRYING PROJECTION OF UPPER
STORY; HOUSE AT YORK, 14TH CENTURY.

BRACKETS CARRYING PORCH-ROOF; ARNOLD
HOUSE, CHARLESTOWN, MASS.

BRACKETS IN THE OLD CLOISTERS, WINDSOR
CASTLE.

BRICKWORK: WINDOW AT COCCAGLIO, LOMBARDY,
ITALY, 14TH CENTURY.

BRICKWORK: ARCHIVOLT
AT CREMONA.

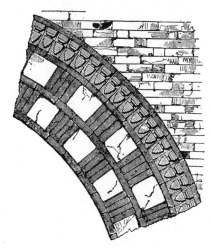

BRICKWORK: ARCHIVOLT IN THE BISHOP'S PALACE,
MANTUA.

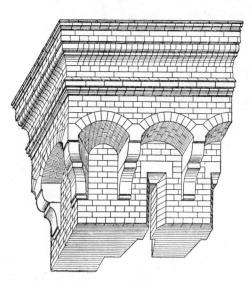

BRICKWORK: MODERN WALL-CORNICE, WITH
ARCHES RESTING ON TERRA-COTTA CORBELS.

BRICKWORK: MODERN CHURCH, NŒUX-LES-MINES, NEAR CALAIS, FRANCE.

BRIDGE (ROMAN) AT ALCÁNTARA, SPAIN.

BRIDGE UNITING TWO PALAZZI AT FOLIGNO, ITALY.

BRIDGE OF VALENDRÉ, WITH FORTIFIED TOWERS, AT CAHORS, SOUTHWESTERN FRANCE.

BROLETTO AT COMO, LOMBARDY.

BROLETTO AT MONZA, LOMBARDY.

BUSH HAMMER.

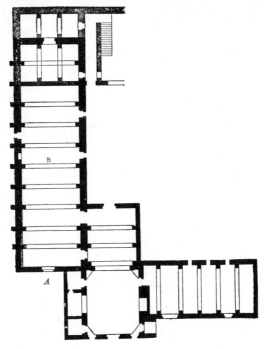

BUTTRESS: FIG. 1. — AN EARLY FORM; THE MASS
PARTLY WITHIN AND PARTLY BEYOND THE
WALLS. PALACE AT CHAQQA, SYRIA.

See Fig. 2, partial section, showing transverse arches, *B;* and
Fig. 3, partial end wall at *A.*

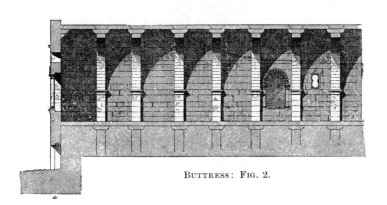

BUTTRESS: FIG. 2.

BUTTRESS: FIG. 3.

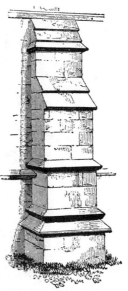

BUTTRESS OF AISLE
WALL: WARMINGTON
CHURCH, NORTHAMP-
TONSHIRE, C. 1260.

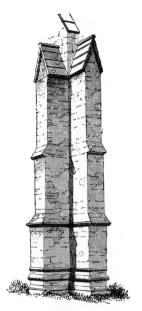

BUTTRESS: TWO AT ANGLE
OF AISLE; OXFORD CA-
THEDRAL, C. 1330.

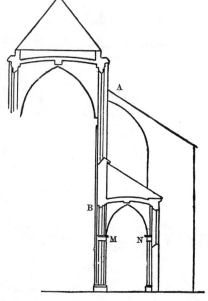

FLYING BUTTRESS: DIAGRAM SHOWING ACTION.

A. The flying buttress. *F.* The open space beneath arch of
flying buttress. *B.* The crown of one of the arches supporting clerestory wall. *M N.* Arch across the aisle, which
would have been loaded too heavily but for the opening
above, *F.*

FLYING BUTTRESS:
HARTLEPOOL CHURCH,
DURHAM, C. 1250.

FLYING BUTTRESS: STRASBURG CATHEDRAL; NORTH SIDE OF NAVE.

The perfected system, with heavy buttress piers.

FLYING BUTTRESS: SAINT DENIS, C. 1240.
Radiating system of rounded or polygonal east end; apsidal chapels between the buttress piers.

FLYING BUTTRESS: CHURCH OF S. REMY AT REIMS (MARNE), FRANCE.
Diagram of arrangement of double-aisled church with two flying buttress systems.

**BUTTRESS PIER: CHAPTER HOUSE, LINCOLN,
C. 1270.**

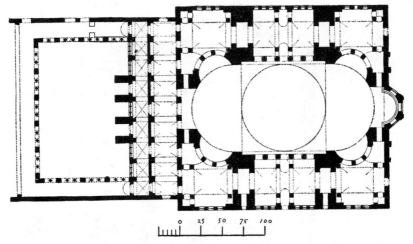

BYZANTINE ARCHITECTURE: CHURCH OF S. SOPHIA (PLAN) AT CONSTANTINOPLE; AS REBUILT, 538 AND 558.

BYZANTINE ARCHITECTURE: CHURCH OF S. SOPHIA. (SECTION.)

(See plan.)

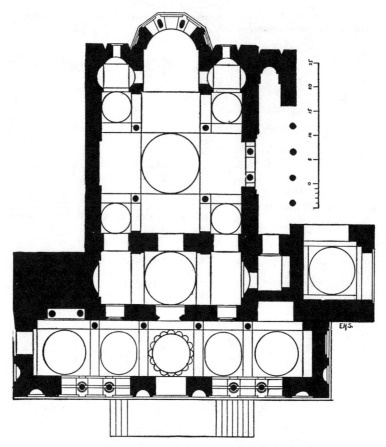

BYZANTINE ARCHITECTURE: CHURCH OF THE THEOTOKOS (*A*, PLAN), CONSTANTINOPLE; 10TH CENTURY.

BYZANTINE ARCHITECTURE: CHURCH OF THE THEOTOKOS (*B*, ELEVATION; SEE *A*, PLAN).

CALVARY AT PLOUGASTEL, NEAR BREST IN BRITTANY.

CAMPANILE: CHURCH OF S. GIORGIO AL VELABRO, ROME; 7TH OR 8TH
CENTURY.

CAMPANILE: CATHEDRAL OF CREMONA, LOMBARDY; CALLED IL TORRAZZO (THE GREAT TOWER), AS BEING THE HIGHEST IN ITALY — ABOUT 400 FEET; c. 1280.

CAMPANILE: PALAZZO SCALIGERI, VERONA.

CAMPANILE: CHURCH OF S. MARIA MAGGIORE, BERGAMO, LOMBARDY; 14TH CENTURY, EXCEPT THE WOODEN ROOF.

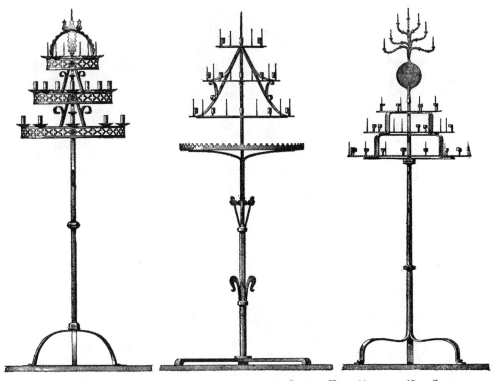

CANDELABRUM: THREE WROUGHT-IRON CANDELABRA FOR CHURCH USE; 14TH AND 15TH CENTURIES.

CANDELABRUM OF MARBLE; BAPTISTERY, FLORENCE.

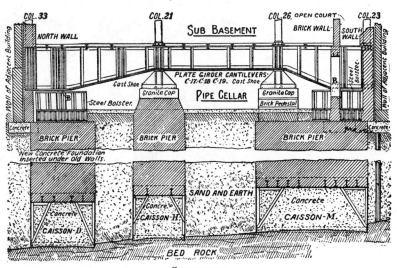

CANTILEVER.

79

CAPITAL: LOTUS BUD CAPITAL FROM TEMPLE AT LUXOR.

CAPITAL: PAPYRUS CAPITAL FROM RAMESSEUM, THEBES.

CAPITAL FROM THE TEMPLE OF KARNAK.

CAPITAL: HATHOR CAPITAL AT DENDERAH, UPPER EGYPT.

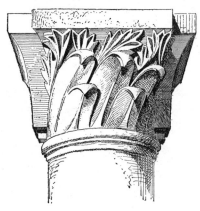

CAPITAL FROM BETOURSA, SYRIA.

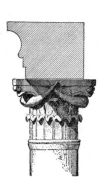

CAPITALS FROM HOUSES NEAR SERDJILLA, SYRIA; C. 400 A.D.

CAPITAL WITH GREAT PROJECTION IN THE PLANE OF THE WALL ABOVE, THUS AFFORDING A LARGE BEARING FOR THE LINTELS. FROM BAGOUZA, SYRIA.

CAPITAL FROM TOMB IN NORTH SIDE OF CHOIR, CATHEDRAL OF ROUEN.

CAPITAL: CORNER CAPITAL FROM TEMPLE OF ATHENA NIKE; CLOSE OF 5TH CENTURY, B.C.

CAPITAL: IONIC CORNER CAPITAL FROM ERECHTHEUM.

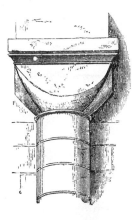

CAPITAL: SHAFT FROM NORTH TRANSEPT, WINCHESTER CATHEDRAL.

CAPITAL: S. NICOLAS, BLOIS; C. 1200.

CAPITAL: SOISSONS CATHEDRAL; C. 1212.

CAPITAL: NORMAN
CUSHION CAPI-
TAL; CASSINGTON,
OXFORDSHIRE.

CAPITAL: NORMAN;
STEETLEY, DER-
BYSHIRE.

CAPITAL: EARLY
ENGLISH; HAMP-
TON POYLE, OXON.

CAPITAL: EARLY
ENGLISH, HASE-
LEY, OXON.

CAPITAL: PRESBYTERY, LINCOLN; c. 1260.

CAPITAL: CHAPTER HOUSE, SOUTHWELL.

CAPITAL: HARRINGTON, NORTHAMPTONSHIRE; c. 1300.

CARTOUCHE: CARVING IN WOOD; CHÂTEAU D'ANET.

CARVING: PANEL FROM THE CLUNY MUSEUM.

CARYATID PORCH (SO-CALLED), SOUTH SIDE OF ERECHTHEUM, ATHENS.

CASA GRANDE: GROUND PLAN AND SKETCH OF
WALLS.

CASTLE: LITTLE WENHAM HALL, SUFFOLK; 13TH CENTURY. (SEE PLAN.)

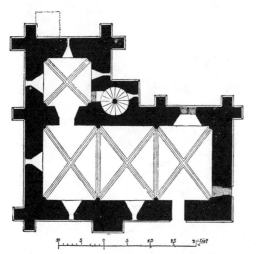

CASTLE: PLAN OF LITTLE WENHAM HALL,
SUFFOLK.

CASTLE AT COCA, NEAR SEGOVIA, SPAIN; 15TH CENTURY.

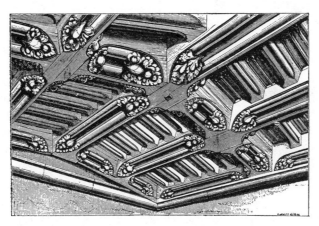

CEILING OF CARVED WOOD IN NAWORTH CASTLE, CUMBERLAND;
14TH CENTURY.

CEILING OF STONE SLABS CARRIED ON HORIZONTAL RIBS, SUPPORTED BY ARCHES; CHURCH
AT TILLIÈRES (EURE), FRANCE; SECOND HALF OF 16TH CENTURY. (SEE PLAN.)

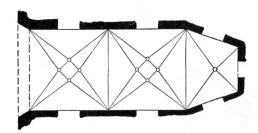

CEILING: APPROXIMATE PLAN OF CEILING AT TILLIÈRES, SHOWN IN CUT.

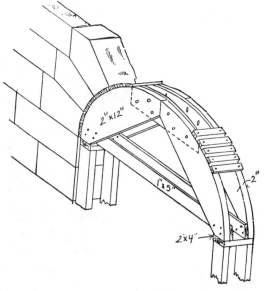

CENTRING FOR AN ARCHED OPENING OF SMALL
SPAN.

Certosa, near Pavia Lombardy, Italy.

Certosa, near Pavia: Detail of the Front of
the Church; about 1475 a.d.

CHAPEL IN SOUTH AISLE OF CHOIR, CHURCH AT NORREY (CALVADOS), FRANCE.

CHAPEL : CHAPELLE DE L'EVÊQUE, PÉRIGUEUX (DORDOGNE), FRANCE.

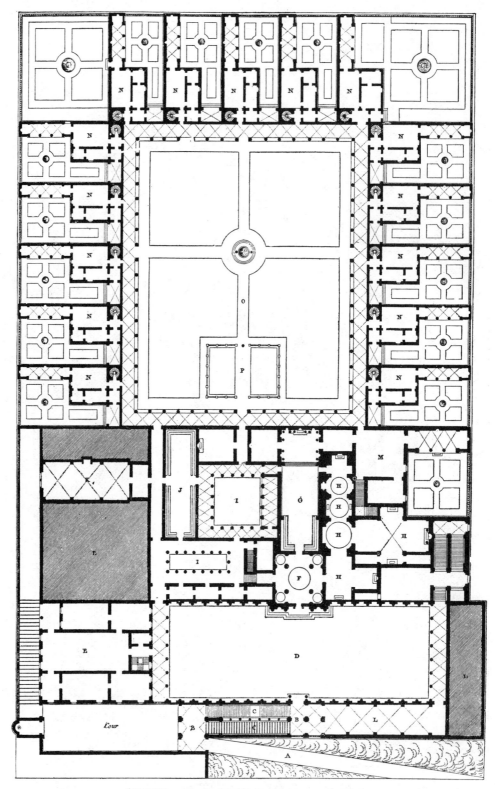

CERTOSA: PLAN OF THAT NEAR FLORENCE.

A. Road of approach to the lobbies *B*. *B*. Vaulted lobbies of entrance. *C*. Stairs leading to upper story. *D*. Outer court, giving access to vestibule *F*. *E*. Residence of the Superior. *F*. Vestibule leading to the monastery proper. *G*. Church. *I*. Small cloister. *H, J, K, L, M*. Buildings of administration, kitchens, bake-houses, lodgings for strangers and the like. *N*. Monks' cells. *O*. Cloister. *P*. Lavatory.

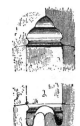

CHAMFERS WITH ORNAMENTAL STOPS.

A. At Exton Church, Rutland. *B*. At Glastonbury Abbey. *C*. At Courtlodge,
Godmersham, Kent. *D*. Cross section of chamfer.

CHANCEL OF STAINDROP CHURCH, YORKSHIRE; ABOUT
1370 A.D.

Perpendicular style. The end window somewhat later.

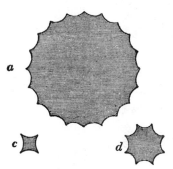

CHANNELING.

a. Showing in plan the typical Doric column. *d*. Plan of a
shaft in the cathedral at Monza, Lombardy, Italy. *c*. A
section rare in architecture, except occasionally in late
Gothic.

CHAPEL OF CHOIR, CATHEDRAL OF LE MANS (SARTHE), FRANCE.

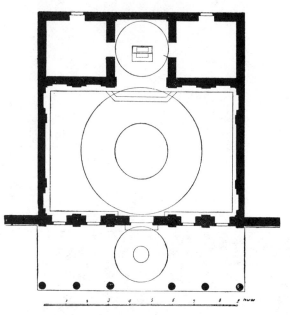

CHAPEL OF THE PAZZI: PLAN. (SEE CUT.)

CHAPEL OF THE PAZZI, CHURCH OF S. CROCE, FLOR-
ENCE, ITALY. (SEE PLAN.)

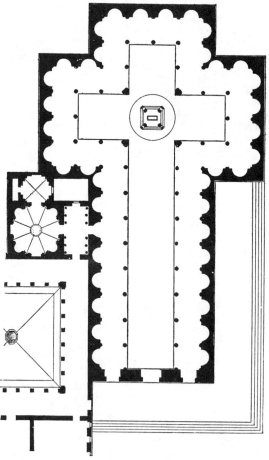

CHAPEL: CHURCH OF S. SPIRITO, FLORENCE, WITH
NICHES USED AS CHAPELS IN THE OUTER WALLS.

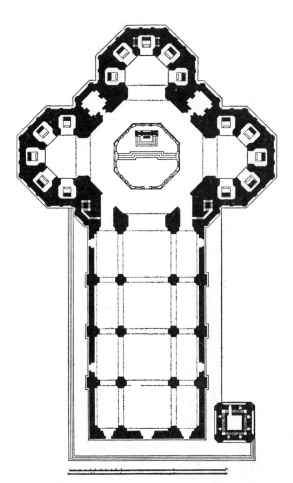

CHAPEL: CATHEDRAL OF FLORENCE, WITH
FIFTEEN APSIDAL CHAPELS FORMING
EXTERNALLY A LARGER AND LOWER OC-
TAGONAL PROJECTION OF EACH APSE.

DOMESTIC CHAPEL, BROUGHTON CASTLE, OXFORDSHIRE;
THE EAST END.

93

CHAPTER HOUSE OF THE CATHEDRAL OF NOYON (OISE), FRANCE; WEST SIDE.

CHAPTER ROOM OF SALISBURY CATHEDRAL.

CHÂTEAU OF THE FRENCH RENAISSANCE: CENTRAL MASS OF CHAMBORD; 1525 TO 1540. (SEE PLAN.)

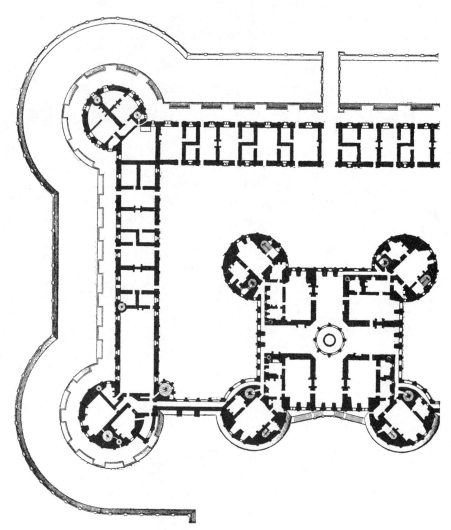

CHÂTEAU OF CHAMBORD. (SEE CUT.)

CHEVET OF COUTANCES CATHEDRAL; GENERAL VIEW FROM THE
BISHOP'S GARDENS.

CHEVRON MOULDING: CHAPTER HOUSE, CHRIST
CHURCH, OXFORD.

CHEVET OF THE CATHEDRAL OF CHÂLONS-SUR-MARNE; INTERIOR VIEW, LOOKING EAST.

CHIMNEY AND BATTLEMENT, CREMONA.

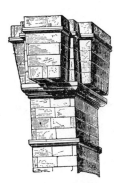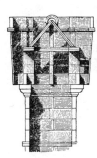

CHIMNEY OF THE MILL OF MANNEBERG, SWITZER-
LAND.

Constructed of thin tiles set on edge to insure the least weight
possible on the wooden framework which supports it.

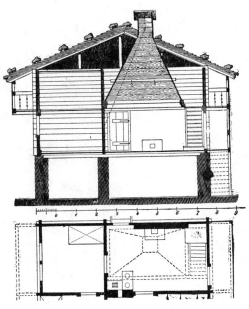

CHIMNEY OF A HOUSE IN MEININGEN, SWITZER-
LAND.

Consisting of a wooden hood covering nearly the entire kitchen,
and having a movable cover operated from below.

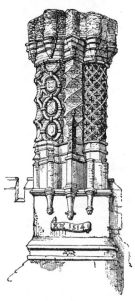

CHIMNEY: THORNBURY
CASTLE, GLOUCESTER-
SHIRE, C. 1514 A.D.

CHIMNEY IN RIO DI
CASTEL FORTE,
VENICE.

CHIMNEY OF PALAZZO
ALBRIZZI, VENICE.

CHIMNEY OF PALAZZO
DELLA ZECCA, VENICE.

CHIMNEY FROM ARCHBISHOP'S PALACE, SOUTH-
WELL, NOTTINGHAMSHIRE.

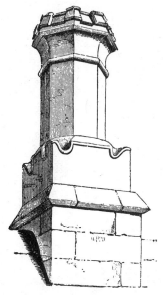

CHIMNEY AT EXTON, RUTLAND, ENG-
LAND, C. 1350.

CHIMNEY PIECE OF THE CHÂTEAU OF VILLEROI; NOW IN THE
LOUVRE.

5 4 3 2 1 0

CHORAGIC MONUMENT OF LYSICRATES, ATHENS; RESTORATION BY STUART AND REVET. (SEE CUT, COL. 551.)

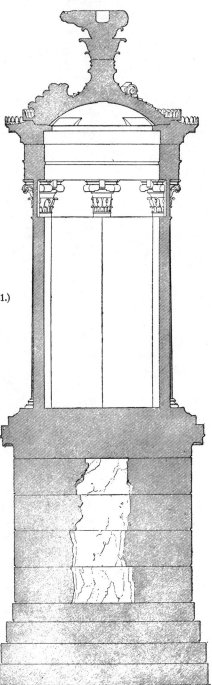

CHORAGIC MONUMENT OF LYSICRATES, ATHENS, GREECE. (SEE CUT, COLS. 549, 550.)

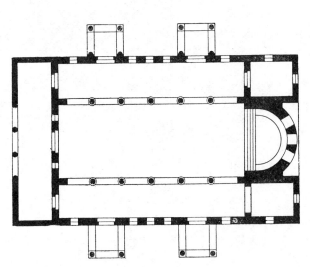

CHURCH AT BAQOUZA, SYRIA: 6TH CENTURY. (SEE SECTION AND CUT, COLS. 555, 556.)

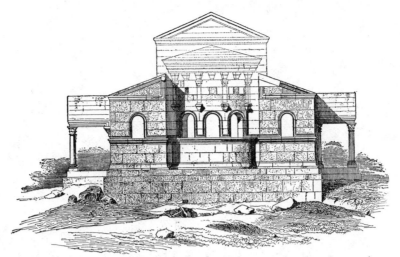

CHURCH AT BAQOUZA, SYRIA; 6TH CENTURY. (SEE PLAN AND SECTION.)

CHURCH AT BAQOUZA, SYRIA; 6TH CENTURY. (SEE PLAN AND CUT.)

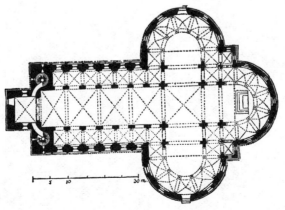

CHURCH OF S. MARTIN, COLOGNE.

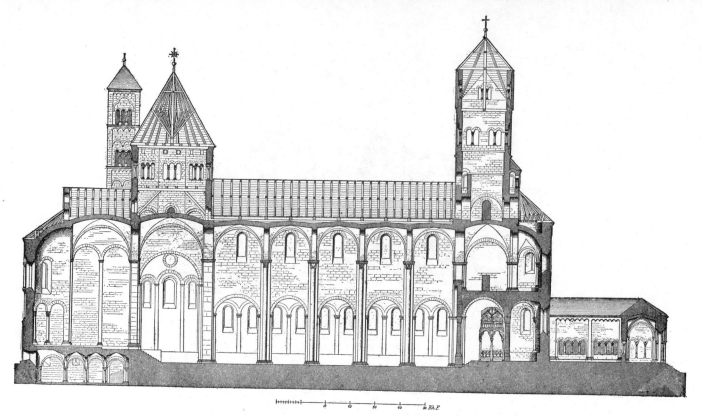

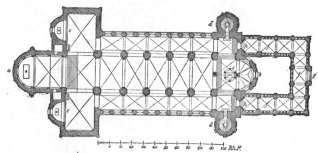

ABBEY CHURCH,
LAACH, GERMANY,
12TH CENTURY.
(SEE CUT, COLS. 561, 562.)

104

ABBEY CHURCH, LAACH. (SEE PLAN AND SECTION, COLS. 559, 560.)

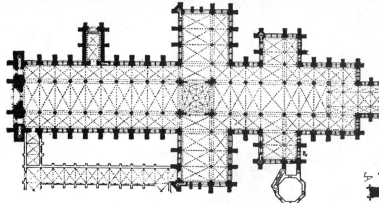

CHURCH: PLAN OF SALISBURY CATHEDRAL; TWO TRANSEPTS.

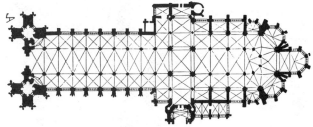

CHURCH OF S. OUEN: PLAN AS ORIGINALLY BEGUN (1320–1350).
West end with towers set diagonally. The chapels are later.

CHURCH OF S. PETRONIO AT BOLOGNA: NAVE; CLOSE OF
14TH CENTURY.

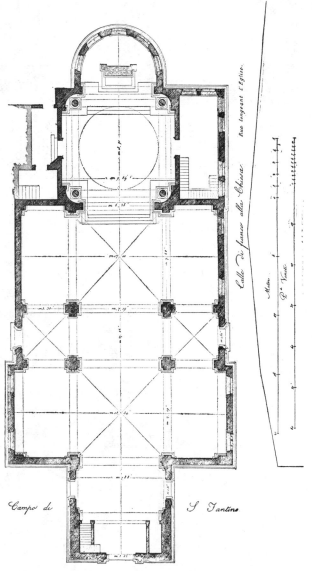

CHURCH OF S. FANTINO, VENICE; 1510–1533.

105

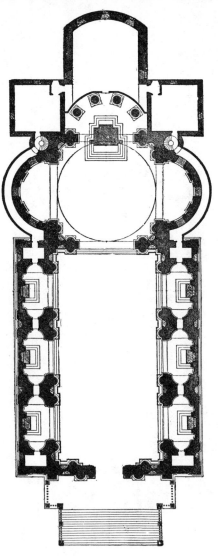

CHURCH OF S. REDENTORE, VENICE.

CHURCH OF S. PETER: PART OF NORTH FRONT, SHOWING CHOIR (TURNED
TO THE WEST). NORTHERN APSE. COLOSSAL ORDER AND ATTIC;
ALL OF 1536. CUPOLA OF CIRCA 1590.

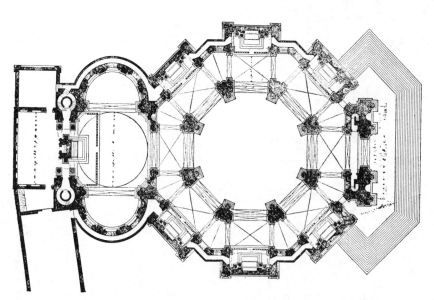

CHURCH OF S. MARIA DELLA SALUTE, VENICE.

CHURCH OF S. PAUL: SOUTH PART OF WEST FRONT.

CHURCH OF S. PAUL IN LONDON: SECTION THROUGH CUPOLA, SHOWING INNER CUPOLA, BRICK CONE, AND WOODEN OUTER SHELL; STONE LANTERN RESTING ON BRICK CONE. WORK OF SIR CHRISTOPHER WREN, 1680 TO 1710 A.D.

CHURCH OF S. ROCH, PARIS: NAVE; CIRCA 1660 A.D.

CHURCH: FORTIFIED CHURCH, MÜNSTER MAIFELD, GERMANY.

CINQUE CENTO DESIGN: PALAZZO DEI CONSERVATORI AT ROME; CLOSING YEARS OF 16TH CENTURY.

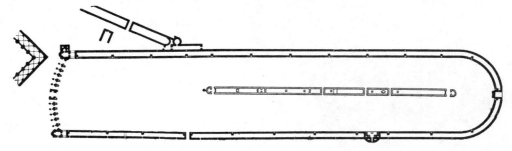

CIRCUS OF MAXENTIUS, NEAR ROME, ITALY.

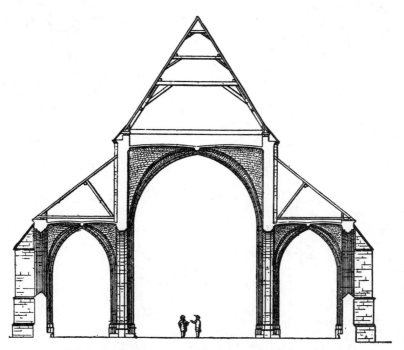

CLEARSTORY, FIG. 1: CHURCH OF VILVORDE, BELGIUM.

What should have been the clearstory is covered by aisle roof (see Fig. 2).

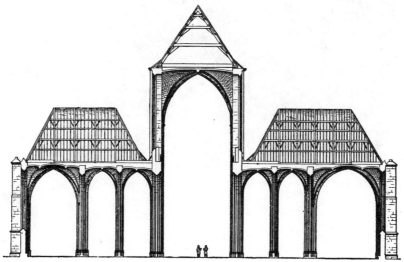

CLEARSTORY, FIG. 2: CATHEDRAL OF ANTWERP, BELGIUM.

The aisles covered by a roof hipped so as to leave open the clearstory.

CLIFF DWELLINGS: A RUINED VILLAGE.

CLIFF DWELLING RUIN.

CLOISTER: CATHEDRAL OF NOYON (OISE): VIEW OF EAST SIDE OF CHAPTER HOUSE AND PART OF CLOISTER.

CLOISTER: CARMINE CONVENT, BRESCIA.

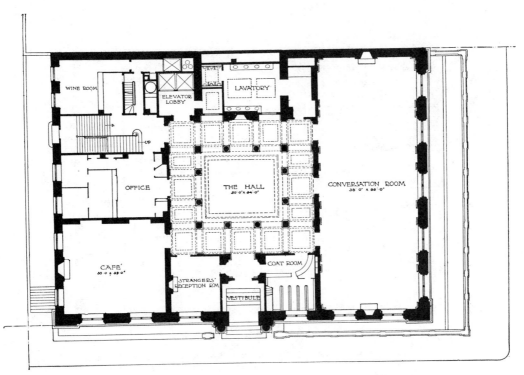

CLUB HOUSE: UNIVERSITY CLUB, NEW YORK; GROUND FLOOR.

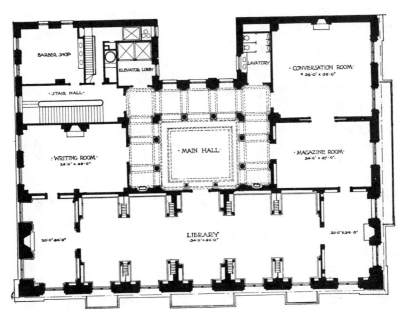

CLUB HOUSE: UNIVERSITY CLUB, NEW YORK; SECOND PRINCIPAL FLOOR.

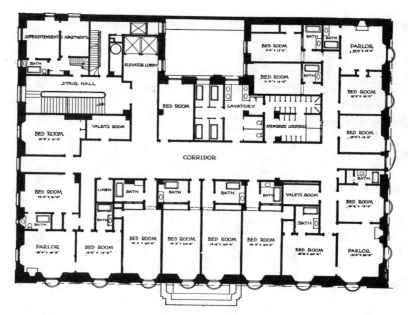

CLUB HOUSE: UNIVERSITY CLUB, NEW YORK; ONE OF THE TWO MEZZANINES.

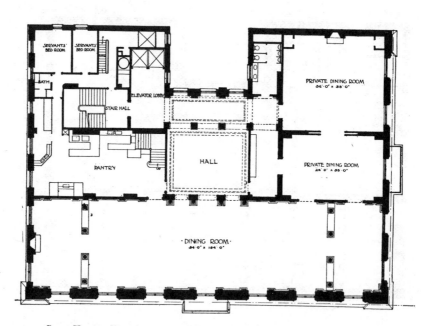

CLUB HOUSE: UNIVERSITY CLUB, NEW YORK; THIRD PRINCIPAL FLOOR.

CLUB HOUSE: UNIVERSITY CLUB, NEW YORK. (SEE PLANS.)

CLUSTERED PIERS: NORWICH CATHEDRAL, C. 1100.

CLUSTERED PIER: COGENHOE, NORTHAMPTON-
SHIRE.

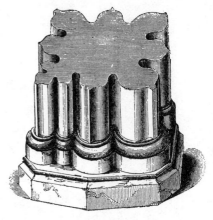

CLUSTERED PIER: S. MARY'S ABBEY, YORK,
c. 1250.

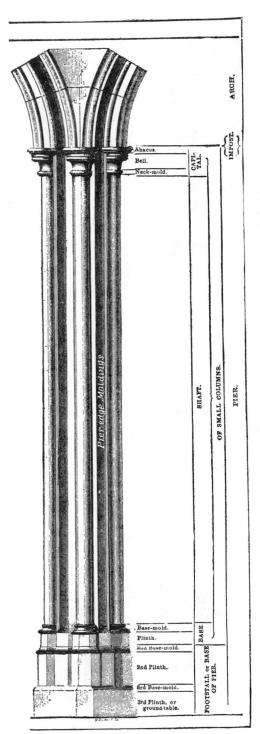

CLUSTERED PIER.

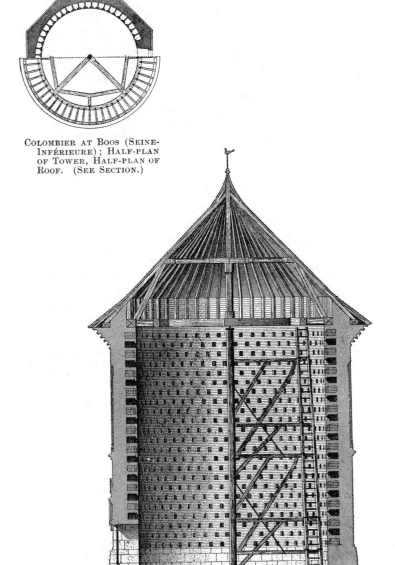

COLOMBIER AT BOOS (SEINE-
INFÉRIEURE); HALF-PLAN
OF TOWER, HALF-PLAN OF
ROOF. (SEE SECTION.)

COLOMBIER AT BOOS (SEINE-INFÉRIEURE); CROSS-SECTION.
(SEE PLAN.)

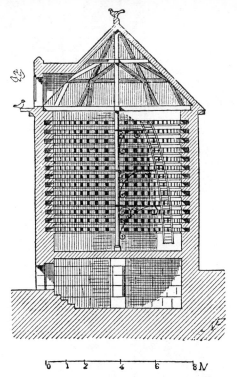

COLOMBIER ON A FARM AT POUGUES (NIÈVRE);
CROSS-SECTION.

COLOMBIER: PROVENCE AND LANGUEDOC;
TYPICAL FORM.

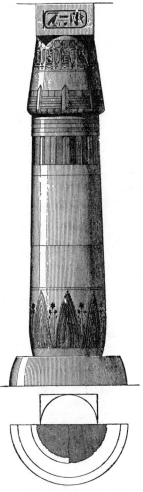

COLUMN OF PAPYRUS-BUD TYPE;
THEBES, EGYPT.

COLUMN: ROMAN; FROM TOMB OF CAIUS-CESTIUS
AT ROME.

COLUMN: SYRIAN ROMANESQUE; PORTICOES OF HOUSES
NEAR SERDJILLA IN SYRIA.

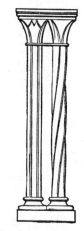

COLUMNS: ITALIAN
ROMANESQUE: OF
S. ZENO, VERONA.

COLUMN: FRENCH RE-
NAISSANCE; CEME-
TERY OF S. MACLOU,
ROUEN.

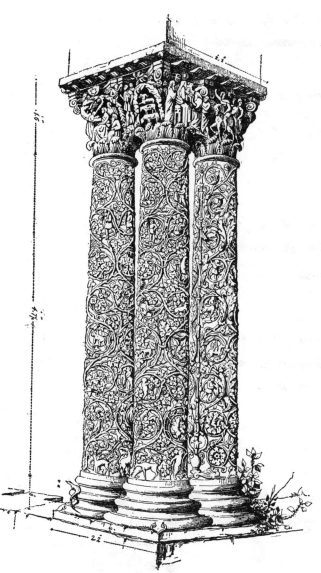

COLUMNS: ITALIAN ROMANESQUE; CLOISTERS,
MONREALE, SICILY, C. 1187.

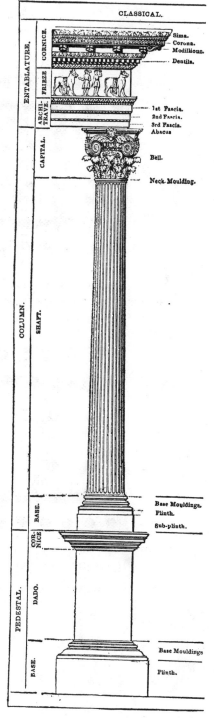

CLASSICAL.

Sima.
Corona.
Modillions.
Dentils.

1st Fascia.
2nd Fascia.
3rd Fascia.
Abacus

Bell.

Neck Moulding.

Base Mouldings.
Plinth.

Sub-plinth.

Base Mouldings

Plinth.

ENTABLATURE. — CORNICE. — FRIEZE. — ARCHITRAVE.

COLUMN. — CAPITAL. — SHAFT. — BASE.

PEDESTAL. — CORNICE. — DADO. — BASE.

COLUMNAR ARCHITECTURE: COMPOSITE ORDER;
NOMENCLATURE OF MEMBERS.

117

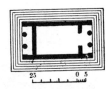

COLUMNAR ARCHITECTURE:
AMPHIPROSTYLE TEM-
PLE; EACH PORTICO DIS-
TYLE IN ANTIS.

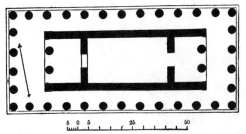

COLUMNAR ARCHITECTURE: SO-CALLED TEMPLE OF
THESEUS, ATHENS; 5TH CENTURY B.C.

Hexastyle peripteral temple; pronaos and epinaos, each distyle
in antis.

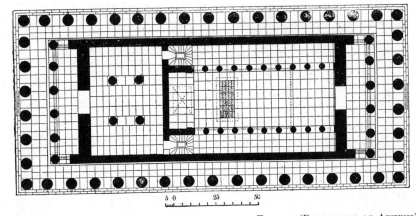

COLUMNAR ARCHITECTURE: OCTASTYLE PERIPTERAL TEMPLE (PARTHENON AT ATHENS).

Two hexastyle porticoes within; epinaos (to left), hypostyle with four columns. Larger division of naos thought by some to
have been partly hypæthral.

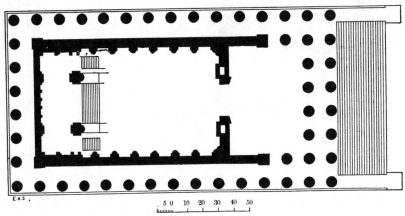

COLUMNAR ARCHITECTURE: OCTASTYLE PERIPTERAL TEMPLE AT BAALBEK IN SYRIA; THE ENTRANCE
PORTICO DIPTERAL.

The shafts of the outer peristyle are smooth; the eight shafts within are fluted and form a pronaos with its own entablature.

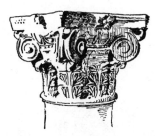

COMPOSITE: EARLIEST USE OF
IT IN ARCH OF TITUS.

COMPOSITE CAPITAL IN LATERAN MUSEUM AT ROME.

COMPOSITION: HOUSE OF JACQUES CŒUR, BOURGES; ELEVATION OF FRONT NEXT THE STREET.

CONSOLE: CATHEDRAL OF COMO, LOMBARDY,
ITALY.

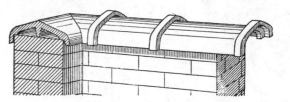

COPING OF TERRA COTTA.

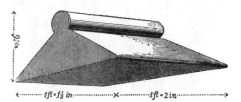

COPING STONE OF A COMMON MEDIÆVAL TYPE.

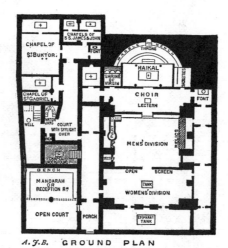

A.J.B. GROUND PLAN

COPTIC CHURCH OF ABU-'S-SIFAIN, AND THE
ADJOINING CHAPELS.

COPTIC: DAIR BABLÛN (IN THE FOREGROUND) AND DAIR TADRUS (BEYOND),
ENCLOSING EACH A CHURCH.

COPTIC CONVENT DAIR-AS-SÛRIÂM, AND NEIGH-
BOURING CONVENT OF ANBA BISHÒI (IN THE
BACKGROUND).

CORBEL IN BROAD-
WATER CHURCH,
SUSSEX.

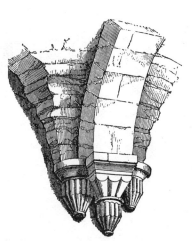

CORBEL AT KIRKSTALL ABBEY, 1150.

CORBEL AT POLEBROOK, NORTHAMPTONSHIRE,
c. 1200.

CORBEL: LINCOLN CATHEDRAL.

CORBEL IN HALL OF
CHRIST CHURCH, OX-
FORD, C. 1529.

CORBELS CARRYING A BATTLEMENTED PARAPET.

CORBELLING IN CLOISTER OF S. PABLO IN
BARCELONA.

CORBEL ARCH IN THE NECROPOLIS OF MOUGHEÏR,
LOWER CHALDEA.

CORBELLING OF A BAY WINDOW IN DIJON, FRANCE.

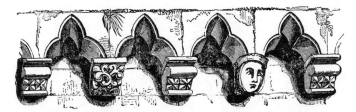

CORBEL TABLE AT ROMSEY CHURCH, HANTS, C. 1200.

CORINTHIAN CAPITAL, APPARENTLY INTENDED FOR THE THOLOS AT EPIDAURUS; C. 300 B.C.

CORINTHIAN CAPITAL OF SIMPLEST TYPE.

Cornice of a House of the 6th Century at Refadi, Syria; formed by the Projection of the Roof Slabs beyond the Entablature.

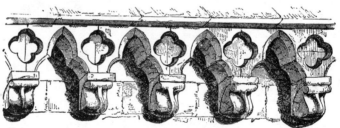

Cornice from Warmington Church, Northamptonshire, c. 1250.

Cornice from Bishop Beekington's Chantry, Wells Cathedral, c. 1465.

CORNICE, S. FRANCESCO,
BRESCIA, ITALY.

CORNICE FORMED BY THE ORNAMENTAL TREATMENT OF THE ROOF FRAMING.

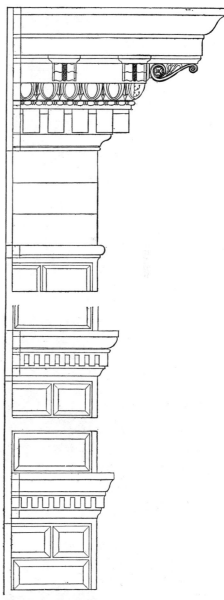

CORNICIONE FROM THE
PALAZZO STROZZI,
FLORENCE, ITALY.

CORTILE OF THE HOUSE CALLED FORNARINA'S, ROME; THE VESTIBULE, VAULTED, IN THE FOREGROUND.

COURT AT THE FRONT OF A HOUSE IN BRUGES; BUILT C. 1530.

COURT OF HOUSE SITUATED AT THE FOOT OF THE TARPEIAN ROCK; ROME, ITALY.

COURTYARD OF HOUSE OF JACQUES CŒUR, BOURGES.

COURTYARD IN A MOORISH HOUSE IN TANGIERS.

CRANDALL.

CREDENCE FROM CHURCH OF S. CROSS, NEAR WINCHESTER, C. 1460.

CRIB FOR HAY, AT HASLITHALL, SWITZERLAND.

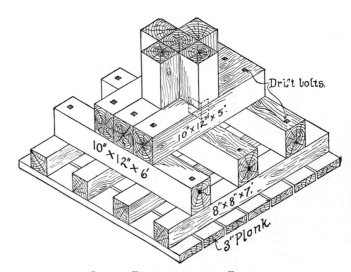

CRIB OF TIMBER, FORMING A FOOTING.

CROCKETS ON A CAPITAL, CA-
THEDRAL OF SEMUR (CÔTE-
D'OR).

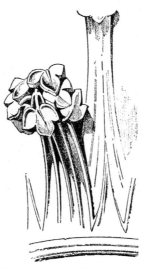

CROCKETS FROM CAPITALS IN
CHOIR, CATHEDRAL OF
SEMUR (CÔTE-D'OR).

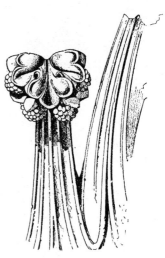

CROCKETS FROM CAPITALS IN CHOIR,
CATHEDRAL OF SEMUR (CÔTE-
D'OR).

CROSSES AS FINIALS OVER GABLES.

CROW STEPS: GLIMMINGEHUS, SCANIA, SWEDEN.

CRYPT: CATHEDRAL OF S. LUCIUS, CHUR, SWITZERLAND.

The choir is approached by the two flights of steps, between which is the entrance to the crypt below.

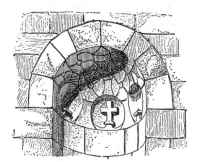

CUL DE FOUR, FORMED BY THE TOP OF A NICHE; CATHEDRAL OF BOSRA, SYRIA.

CUL DE LAMPE (BRACKET); S. STEPHEN'S CHAPEL, WESTMINSTER.

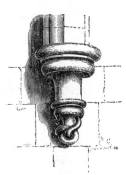

CUL DE LAMPE (BRACK- ET) FROM CHURCH AT EAST DEREHAM, NORFOLK.

130

CUL DE LAMPE.

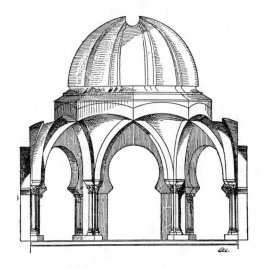

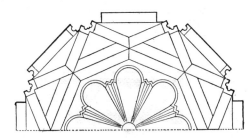

CUPOLA OVER THE MIHRAB OF THE MOSQUE AT
CORDOVA, SPAIN.

CUSP: PART OF THE GENDARMERIE IMPÉRIALE, CAEN
(CALVADOS), FRANCE.

The large windows and one in the turret adorned with solid cusps.

CUSP: EARLY DECORATED;
SOLIHULL CHURCH,
WARWICKSHIRE.

The cusp is pierced, and ends not
in a point but in two reversed
spirals, — a rare form.

CUSP: DOMESTIC WINDOW,
VERONA.

CUSP: GOTHIC TRACERIED WINDOW; LATE 14TH CENTURY (NÔTRE DAME, PARIS).

All the decorative effect being derived from pierced cusps.

CUSP: WINDOW IN S. STEFANO, VENICE.

Double-cusped or double-foliated arch.

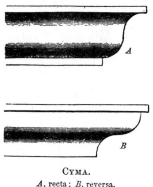

CYMA.

A, recta; B, reversa.

CYMATIUM FROM A HOUSE NEAR SERDJILLA, SYRIA, C. 400 A.D.

CYMATIUM FROM A HOUSE NEAR SERDJILLA, SYRIA, C. 400 A.D.

DALMATIA: DIOCLETIAN'S PALACE AT SPALATO; THE PORTA AUREA OR GILDED GATEWAY.

DALMATIA: PALACE OF DIOCLETIAN AT SPALATO; ARCADE OF GREAT COURT AND ENTRANCE.

DALMATIA: THE DUOMO AT SEBENICO; REMARKABLE FOR STONE ROOF.

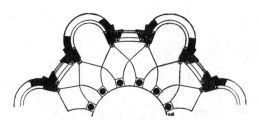

DEAMBULATORY OF NOTRE DAME DU PORT AT
CLERMONT-FERRAND (PUY-DE-DÔME), FRANCE.

DEAMBULATORY: NOTRE DAME DE CHÂLONS (MARNE), FRANCE, 13TH CENTURY.

DEAMBULATORY OF THE CATHEDRAL OF TOLEDO, SPAIN: THE OUTER ONE OF THE TWO AISLES OF THE APSE, 14TH CENTURY.

DECORATED: THE ENGLISH DECORATED STYLE; WINDOW OF S. PETER'S-IN-THE-EAST, OXFORD.

135

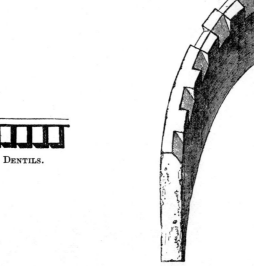

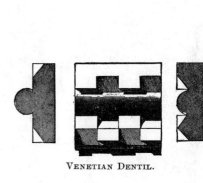

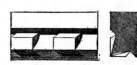

DENTILS.

VENETIAN DENTIL, CUT IN THE HOOD MOULDING OF A WINDOW. DIAGRAM TO SHOW THE METHOD.

VENETIAN DENTIL.

VENETIAN DENTIL.

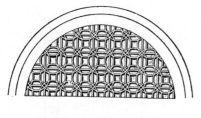

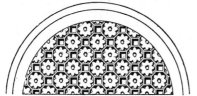

DIAPER: EL-BARAH IN SYRIA; 5TH TO 6TH CENTURY.

DIAPER ON DOORWAY, NORTH SIDE OF CHOIR (PORTE ROUGE), NOTRE DAME, PARIS.

DIAPER FROM THE MONUMENT OF WILLIAM DE VALENCE, WESTMINSTER.

DOGE'S PALACE OF VENICE; SECTION THROUGH THE
SOUTHERN PORTION, FRONTING ON THE RIVA
DEI SCHIAVONI.

A. Ground story, with minor offices (as of police) between
the open arcades *a b* and *c d*. *B.* Second story of small
offices between open arcades. *C.* Great Hall, called Sala
del Maggior Consiglio; about 82 feet wide between the
outer walls; 170 feet long, 21 feet high: garret space above.

DOGE'S PALACE, VENICE; PORTION OF SEA FRONT (SEE SECTION).

DOG-TOOTH MOULDING, KETTON CHURCH,
RUTLAND.

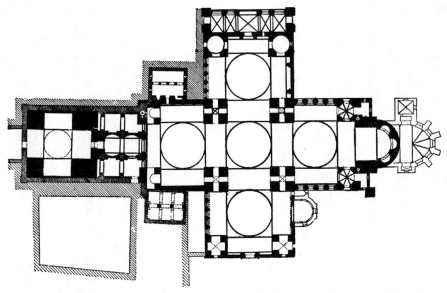

DOMICAL: CHURCH OF S. FRONT, PÉRIGUEUX (DORDOGNE), FRANCE; ROOFED WITH FIVE CUPOLAS.

DOOR OF S. ANASTASIA, VERONA; DECORATIVE
FRAMING IN WOOD.

DOOR OF CARVED WOOD, VENICE; FROM A
PALAZZO OF ABOUT 1550.

DOOR IN THE FAÇADE OF THE CHURCH OF S. GERVAIS, PARIS;
c. 1680.

DOORWAY: THE RATHHAUS, RATISBON (REGENSBURG),
BAVARIA; c. 1662 A.D.

DOORWAY: CHURCH AT GROTTA-FERRATA (LATIUM), ITALY.
The carved marble doorpiece is of unknown early date; the mosaic above is of the 12th century.

DOORWAY: S. MARIA, AT TOSCANELLA (LATIUM), ITALY; EARLY ITALIAN
ROMANESQUE.

DOORWAY: CATHEDRAL OF MAGDEBURG, WESTERN PRUSSIA; C. 122

DOORWAY OF COOMBE CHURCH,
OXON; 14TH CENTURY.

DORMER WINDOW, IN
THE SPIRE, WIT-
NEY, OXFORD-
SHIRE; C. 1240.
EARLY ENGLISH.

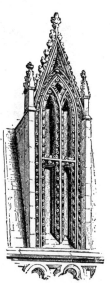

DORMER WINDOW OF
THE DECORATED
STYLE; S. MARY'S,
OXFORD, C. 1300.

140

DORMER WINDOW OF CHAPEL
CLEEVE, SOMERSET; C.
1350.

DORMER IN COURT OF HOTEL DIEU, BEAUNE (CÔTE D'OR),
FRANCE; 1443.

DORMER WINDOW: HOUSE OF JACQUES CŒUR, BOURGES;
1443.

DORMER WINDOWS DETERMINING THE CHARACTER OF A DESIGN. COURTYARD
FRONT, CHÂTEAU OF ÉCOUEN (SEINE-ET-OISE); BEGUN 1545.

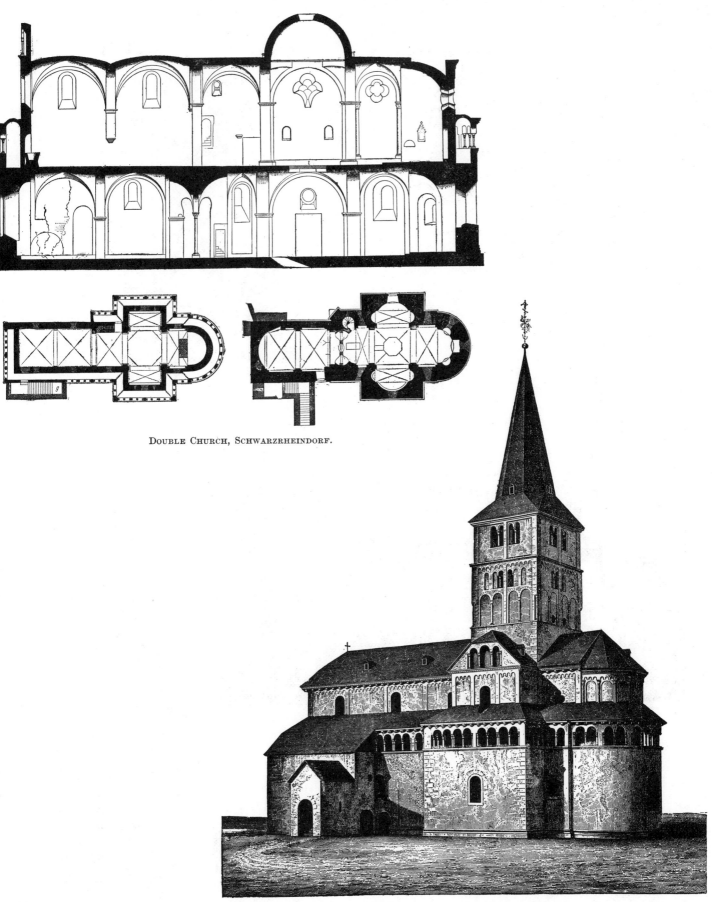

DOUBLE CHURCH, SCHWARZRHEINDORF.

DOUBLE CHURCH, SCHWARZRHEINDORF.

143

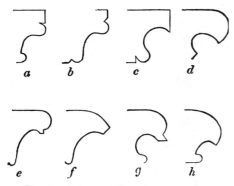

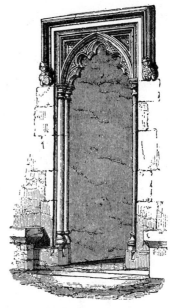

DRIPS FORMED BY MOULDINGS; FROM —

a. The Piazza dei Mercanti, Milan. *b.* The Broletto of Como. *c* and *d.* From Salisbury. *e* and *f.* From Lisieux, Normandy. *g* and *h.* From Wenlock Abbey, Shropshire.

DRIPSTONE FROM S. ERASMUS'S CHAPEL, WEST-MINSTER.

DUCAL PALACE, MANTUA, ITALY.

EAST END: CHURCH OF NORTHBOROUGH, NORTH-AMPTONSHIRE.

Type of simplest form. Compare the photographic plates.

144

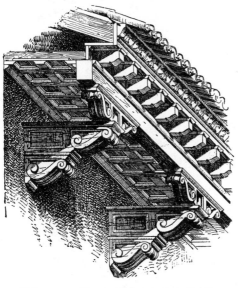

EAVES OF A HOUSE IN SARAGOSSA, SPAIN.

The corbels carry bolsters which support the plate, which carries a course of horizontal timbers partly concealed by a parallel soffit. The rafters receive no support at their ends, beyond the slight steadying effect of the boxing.

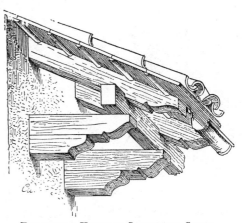

EAVES OF A HOUSE IN SARAGOSSA, SPAIN.

The corbels, each of two horizontal timbers, carry a plate which supports the rafters.

ELIZABETHAN ANGLE TOWER, WOLLATON HALL (NOTTS).

ELIZABETHAN DOORWAY, GAINFORD HALL (DURHAM), c. 1600 A.D.

145

ENGAGED COLUMNS, TEMPLE OF JUPITER, BAALBEK, SYRIA;
PART OF INTERIOR WALL OF CELLA.

ENGLAND: GALILEE OF DURHAM CATHEDRAL; CLOSE OF 12TH CENTURY.

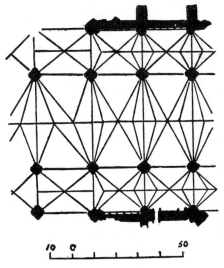

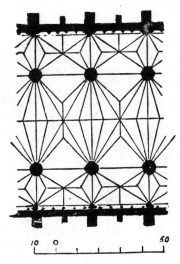

ENGLAND: LINCOLN CATHEDRAL; PLAN OF CHOIR
VAULTING, 1225 A.D.

ENGLAND: LINCOLN CATHEDRAL; PLAN OF NAVE
VAULTING, C. 1235 A.D.

ENGLAND: LINCOLN CATHEDRAL; NAVE VAULTING. (SEE PLAN.)

147

ENGLAND: NORTH AISLE OF CHOIR, CATHEDRAL OF CARLISLE, CUMBERLAND.

Circa 1260, except the window at the right and the arches beneath it, which are perpendicular, of about 1430. They have been removed in the course of recent restoration.

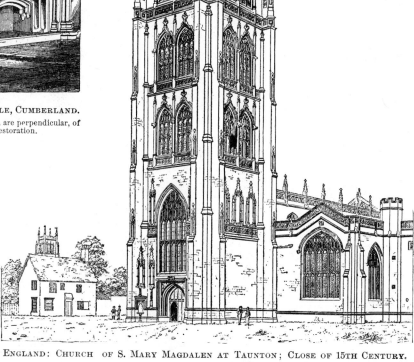

ENGLAND: CHURCH OF S. MARY MAGDALEN AT TAUNTON; CLOSE OF 15TH CENTURY.

England: Beauchamp Chapel, Warwickshire; Late Perpendicular Vaulting, — the First Step
toward Fan Vaulting.

ENTABLATURES OF SIX CLASSIC ORDERS.

1. Tuscan.
2. Grecian Doric.
3. Ionic; Roman Modification.
4. Ionic, Greek type.
5. Corinthian.
6. Composite.

ENTABLATURE OF A PODIUM; INTERIOR STYLOBATE: BASILICA OF THE
ANCIENT PRÆNESTE (NOW PALESTRINA), ITALY.

ENTABLATURE OF LATE ROMAN EPOCH, BENT AROUND AN ARCH: PORTICO
IN DAMASCUS, SYRIA.

ÉPI: WROUGHT LEAD; HOUSE OF JACQUES CŒUR,
BOURGES.

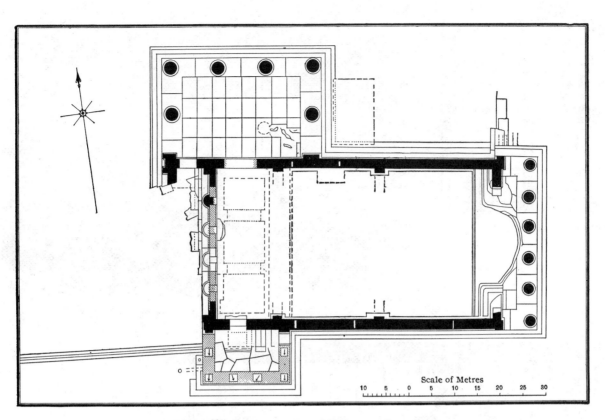

ERECHTHEUM: GROUND PLAN OF EXISTING REMAINS.

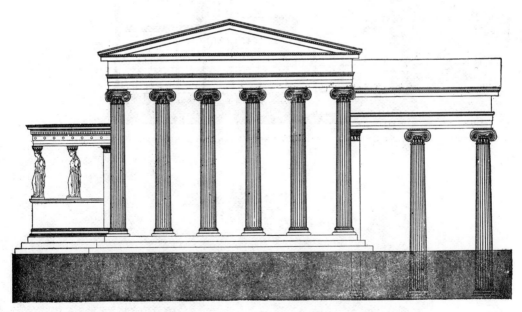

ERECHTHEUM: RESTORED EAST ELEVATION.

The north porch is on much lower ground.   The south porch with caryatids is the famous Pandrosium.

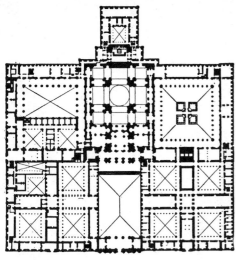

ESCORIAL: GENERAL PLAN.

ESCORIAL. (SEE PLAN.)

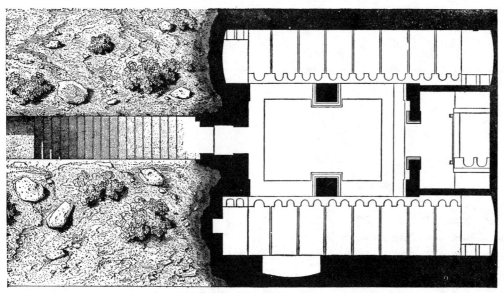

ETRUSCAN TOMB AT CERVETRI (THE ANCIENT CÆRE OF THE ETRUSCANS). PLAN. (SEE SECTION.)

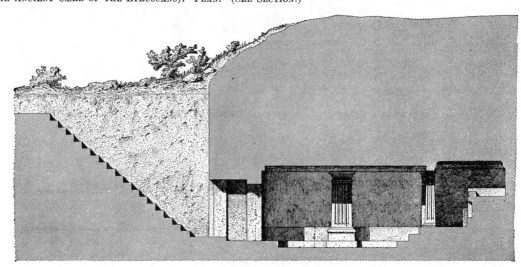

ETRUSCAN TOMB AT CERVETRI (ANCIENT CÆRE). LONGITUDINAL SECTION. (SEE PLAN.)

FAÇADE: CATHEDRAL, CREMONA; NORTH TRANSEPT.
This, having no intimate connection with the side walls, is essentially a façade.

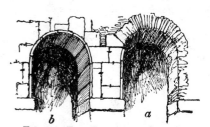

FACING: TWO BYZANTINE STILTED
ARCHES, IN VENICE.
The rough brick work shown in *a* is covered in *b*
by very thin facing of marble.

FACING: GIOTTO'S CAMPANILE, FLORENCE, COVERED WITH
AN ELABORATE FACING OF COLOURED MARBLES.

153

FAN LIGHT OF WOOD AND WROUGHT IRON, FROM A DOORWAY IN PARIS—RUE ANTOINE DUBOIS.

FENESTRATION: PALAZZO ANGARONI-MANZONI, GRAND CANAL, VENICE.
An example of effective design, with many and large openings and little solid wall.

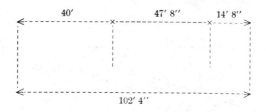

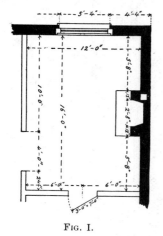

FIG. I.

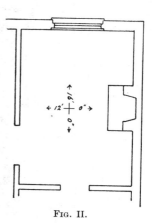

FIG. II.

FIREPLACE IN CHAPTER HOUSE AT NOYON (OISE), C. 1250.
The hood has no side pieces below, but rests on corbels only, so that
the fireplace has no recess.

155

FIREPLACE IN THE HOUSE OF JACQUES CŒUR AT BOURGES (CHER).
The whole is in cut stone; but decorative breasts were often made with plaster on wooden frames.

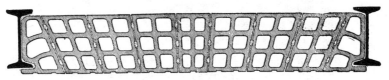

FIREPROOFING. — FIG. 1.
A floor made of voussoir-shaped terra-cotta blocks, forming a flat arch.

FIREPROOFING. — FIG. 2.
A floor made of simpler hollow blocks than those in Fig. 1, and completed by a bed of cement in which sleepers are bedded, and by flooring nailed to those strips; beneath, by plastering.

FLAMBOYANT TRACERY: PORCH OF S. MACLOU,
ROUEN, C. 1460.

FLAMBOYANT TRACERY IN ENGLAND: SALFORD,
WARWICKSHIRE, C. 1360.

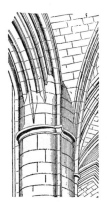

FLAMBOYANT GOTHIC:
PIER AND ARCH-
MOULDINGS, CATHE-
DRAL OF NARBONNE
(AUDE), FRANCE.

FLOOR IN SWISS SOLID TIMBER HOUSE; THE CON-
STRUCTION AND THE FLOORING ALL REPLACED
BY A SYSTEM OF STILES AND PANELS.

FOIL: OPENING
WITH FIVE
FOILS, CALLED
CINQUEFOIL.

FOIL: ARCH WITH FIVE FOILS, CALLED CINQUE-
FOIL ARCH, SALISBURY CATHEDRAL.

FOLIATED CAPITAL, CANTERBURY CATHEDRAL,
c. 1177.

FONT, WITH BLACK MARBLE BOWL, STONE SHAFT, AND BASE: CATHEDRAL,
LAON (AISNE), FRANCE; 12TH CENTURY.

FONT OF BLACK MARBLE, AT NOUVION-LE-VINEUX, NEAR LAON
(AISNE), FRANCE; 12TH CENTURY.

FONT OF STONE, AT URCEL, NEAR LAON (AISNE), FRANCE,
c. 1220.

FONT OF STONE: ENGLISH GOTHIC, c. 1260.

FONT COVER, WHICH, WITH THE FONT, IS OF BRASS; CHURCH OF NOTRE-DAME, HAL,
BELGIUM.

It was cast in 1446.

FORTIFICATION OF ARCHITECTURAL CHARACTER: PART OF THE WORK DEFENDING THE PORTO DEL LIDO, ONE OF THE ENTRANCES TO THE LAGOON OF VENICE; 1544.

FORTIFICATION APPLIED TO A CHURCH: CATHEDRAL OF COIMBRA, PORTUGAL.

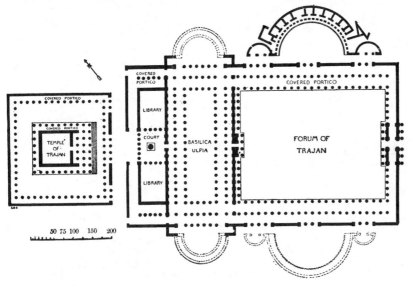

FORUM OF TRAJAN.

Restored plan, with basilica and temple enclosure. The column of Trajan is the object beneath the word "court."

FOUNTAIN OF THE GAT-
TESCHI, VITERBO, IT-
ALY. PLAN.

FOUNTAIN OF THE GATTESCHI, VITERBO, ITALY. (SEE PLAN.)

FOUNTAIN AT AUTUN, NOW DESTROYED; WORK OF
THE EARLY RENAISSANCE.

FRACTABLE: THREE GABLES COPED WITH FRACTA-
BLES; ALL IN SWEDEN.

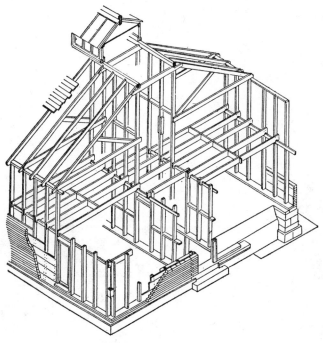

FRAME HOUSE.

The walls and partitions of studs, with interties to carry floor-beams and for stiff-
ness; roof of simple rafters, but with a curb enclosing the opening for a lantern.
This is a German model; and it is shown that an outer shell of brick is intended.

FRANCE, PART I.: NAVE OF ABBEY CHURCH AT VÉZELAY (YONNE); 12TH CENTURY.
The semicircular transverse arches have sunk.

FRANCE, PART I.: NAVE OF CATHEDRAL AT NOYON (OISE).

FRANCE, PART I.: CHARTRES CATHEDRAL; DOOR-WAY, NORTH SIDE OF CLOCK TURRET.

FRANCE, PART III.: CATHEDRAL OF COUTANCES; PART OF NORTH AISLE OF CHOIR.

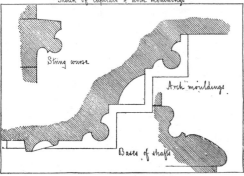

FRANCE, PART III.: CATHEDRAL OF ROUEN; DETAILS OF WINDOW IN UPPER SACRISTY.

FRANCE, PART III.: WINDOWS OF THE HÔTEL BOURG-THEROULDE, ROUEN; EARLY NORMAN RENAISSANCE.

FRANCE, PART III.: COLOMBIER AT BOOS (SEINE-INFÉRIEURE).

See the plan and section under Colombier.

FRANCE, PART VII.: CHURCH OF S. EUTROPIUS,
SAINTES (ON SEASHORE); FLORID ROMANESQUE
CAPITALS.

FRANCE, PART X.: CATHEDRAL OF S. NAZAIRE AT CARCASSONNE (AUDE), SOUTH OF FRANCE,
C. 1320 A.D.

FRANCE, PART I.: CHAPELS, 16TH CENTURY, ATTACHED TO CHURCH OF S. LAURENT,
NOGENT-SUR-SEINE (AUBE).

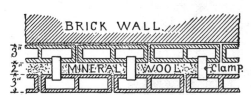

FURRING BY HOLLOW BLOCKS, AS OF TERRA COTTA,
WITH DEAFENING: A VERY ELABORATE SYSTEM.
Compare the cuts under Fireproofing.

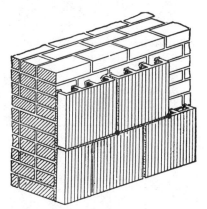

FURRING BY HOLLOW BLOCKS, AS OF TERRA COTTA:
THE SIMPLEST SYSTEM.
The corrugated surface to receive the plaster.

168

GABLE PURELY DECORATIVE: HOUSE AT BEAUVAIS (OISE), FRANCE.

GABLE: HOUSE OF 17TH CENTURY, AT
GHENT, BELGIUM.

The pointed windows and tracery are 14th century
work, restored.

GABLE WITH BLIND TRACERY, 13TH CENTURY; PORCH, CATHE-
DRAL OF AMIENS, SOUTH AISLE.

169

GABLET: East Dereham Church, Norfolk, England.

GALLERY: that at the Triforium level, below; that of the Clearstory Windows, above. Cathedral of Coutances; Bay of East Side of North Transept.

GARDEN HOUSE: Pavilion, 16th Century, at Baux (Bouches du Rhône).

170

GATEWAY: PALAZZO DELLA RAGIONE, MANTUA.

The division of the roof of the passage by the transverse arches
and superimposed walls had originally the purpose of
affording room for defence as by portcullis or by missiles
from above.

GERMANY, PART I. (THE RHINELAND): CAPITALS
FROM WORK OF THE EARLY 12TH CENTURY;
CHURCH AT NEUWEILER, ELSASS.

GERMANY, PART I. (THE RHINELAND): CHURCH
AT BOPPARD, RHENISH PRUSSIA; 12TH CENTURY.

The extremely narrow nave (about 23 feet), the Italian influence visible in the nave arcade, the multifoil window
openings in the vault, and the odd arrangement of the ribs
in this vault, are all noticeable.

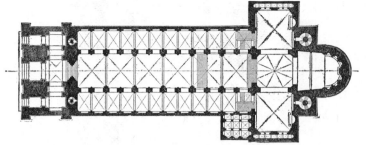

GERMANY, PART II. (THE RHINELAND): CATHEDRAL OF SPEYER (SPIRES),
RHENISH BAVARIA. PLAN.

GERMANY, PART I. (THE RHINELAND): CATHE-
DRAL AT SPEYER; LONGITUDINAL SECTION. (SEE
PLAN.)

This is typical German work, and shows the highest reach of
constructional excellence of the pure Romanesque style.

GERMANY, PART I. (THE RHINELAND): CATHEDRAL OF SPEYER; EXTERIOR.
(SEE PLAN.)

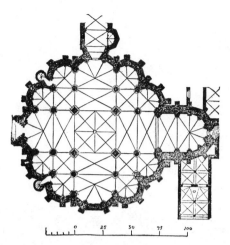

GERMANY, PART I. (THE RHINELAND): CHURCH OF
OUR LADY, AT TREVES (TRIER), C. 1230.
Unique among Gothic churches in its plan.

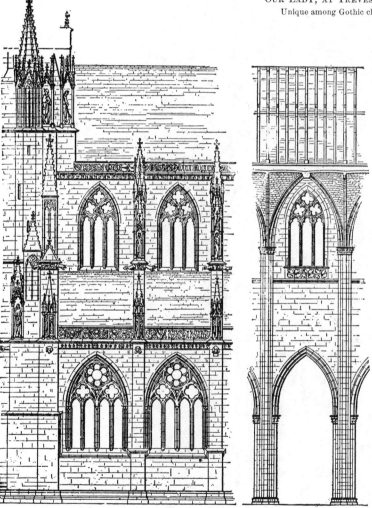

GERMANY, PART I. (THE RHINELAND): MINSTER AT FREIBURG, BADEN, C. 1275.
Two bays and part of tower, south flank; one bay of nave, interior.

GERMANY, PART I. (THE RHINELAND): MINSTER
AT FREIBURG, BADEN; DOORWAY OF THE SAC-
RISTY.

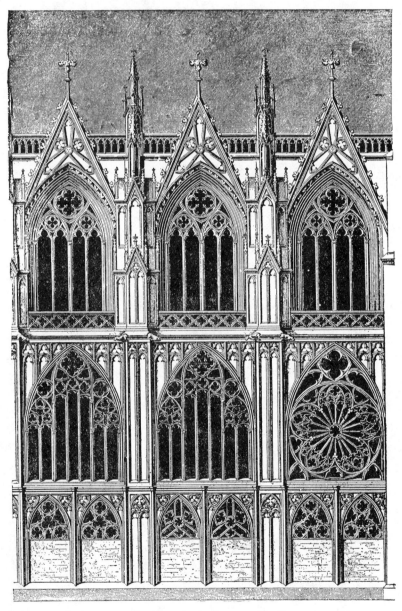

GERMANY, PART I. (THE RHINELAND): S. CATHERINE'S CHURCH AT OPPENHEIM,
HESSE; SOUTH FLANK, C. 1300 A.D.

GERMANY, PART I. (THE RHINELAND): RATHHAUS AT COLOGNE; EARLY GERMAN
RENAISSANCE.

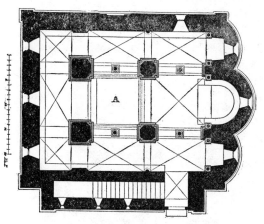

GERMANY, PART II.: CHAPEL OF THE CASTLE OF
LANDSBERG, SAXONY.

A double chapel, with opening in floor to connect the two.

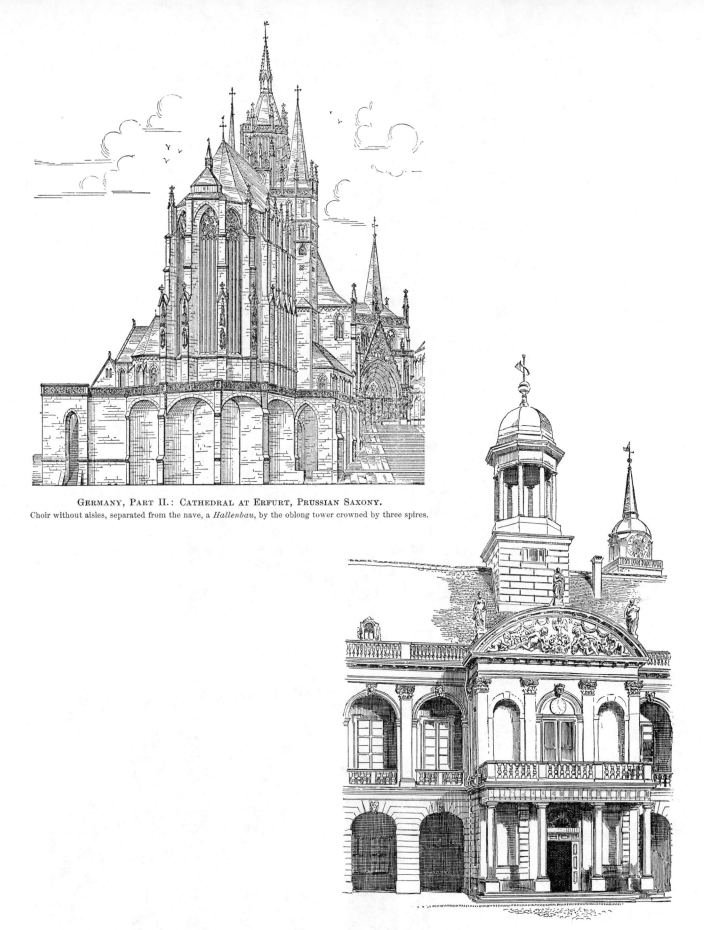

GERMANY, PART II.: CATHEDRAL AT ERFURT, PRUSSIAN SAXONY.
Choir without aisles, separated from the nave, a *Hallenbau*, by the oblong tower crowned by three spires.

GERMANY, PART II.: RATHHAUS AT MAGDEBURG, SAXONY; c. 1690.

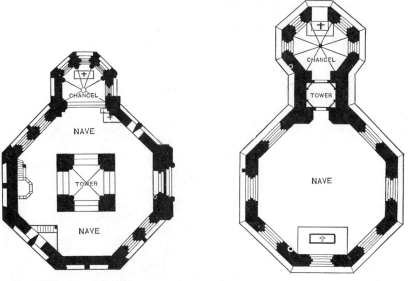

GERMANY, PART III.: OCTAGONAL CHURCHES OF WITTIGSHAUSEN, WITH SQUARE CENTRAL TOWER, AND
GRÜNFELDSHAUSEN [OR GRUENFELDSHAUSEN], BOTH IN BAVARIA; SEE DESCRIPTION IN TEXT.

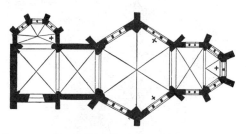

GERMANY, PART III.: CHURCH OF S. CATHERINE,
AT RATISBON; UNIQUE VAULTING.

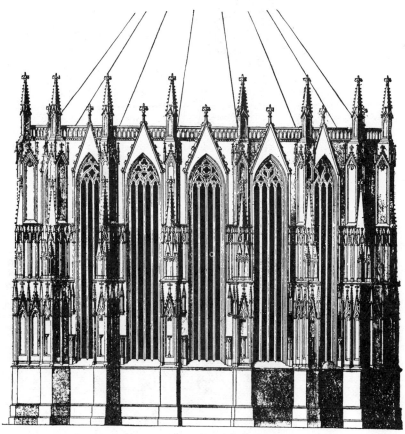

GERMANY, PART III.: CHURCH OF S. SEBALDUS, BAVARIA; EAST END; C. 1375.
The whole eastern choir is a three-aisled *Hallenbau*.

177

GERMANY, PART III.: CHURCH OF OUR LADY AT
ESSLINGEN; SPIRE, EARLY 15TH CENTURY.

GERMANY, PART III.: ST. MICHAEL'S CHURCH, MUNICH, BAVARIA; INTERIOR OF NAVE; C. 1585.

GERMANY, PART III.: VILLA CALLED SOLITUDE, NEAR STUTTGART; C. 1767.

GIBBS, JAMES: CHURCH OF S. MARY ɪ E STRAND,
LONDON; THE SPIRE; C. 1717.

GERMANY, PART IV.: ZEUGHAUS AT DANZIG, EASTERN PRUSSIA;
C. 1605.

GOTHIC ARCHITECTURE (DEFINITION A): CAPITALS
OF SPAIN BEFORE THE MOORISH CONQUEST.

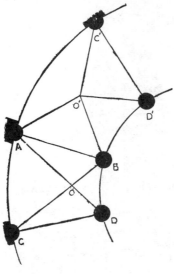

GOTHIC ARCHITECTURE:
FIG. 1.

Diagram of vaulting of circular
deambulatory.

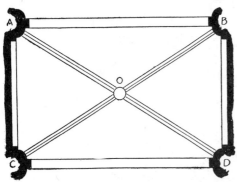

GOTHIC ARCHITECTURE: FIG. 2.

Plan of one compartment of a Gothic vault, *A O* being one
half rib, *A O D* a whole diagonal rib; *A O D, C O B* forming the *croix d'ogires* and *O* the boss or *clef*; *A B, C D,*
transverse arches; *A C, B D,* wall arches (formerets).

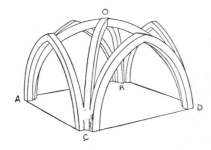

GOTHIC ARCHITECTURE: FIG. 3.

Diagram of ribs corresponding with Fig. 2.

GOTHIC ARCHITECTURE: FIG. 4. THE SAINTE-CHAPELLE FROM THE
SOUTHWEST; 1243–1247 A.D.

180

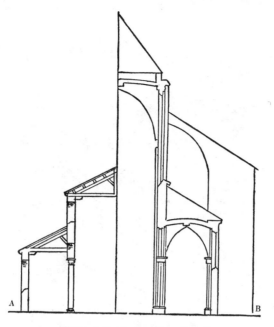

GOTHIC ARCHITECTURE: FIG. 5.

A, half section of early basilica with tie-beam roofs; *B*, half
section of Gothic church with vaulting and flying buttresses.
Both buildings on the same ground plan.

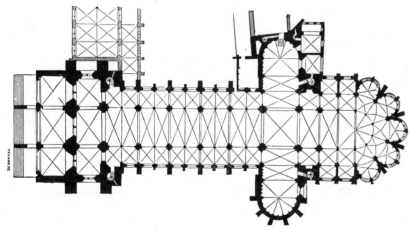

GOTHIC ARCHITECTURE: FIG. 6. CATHEDRAL OF NOYON (OISE), FRANCE.

Transept peculiar in having two rounded ends.　Elaborate vaulting of deambulatory and apsidal chapels.

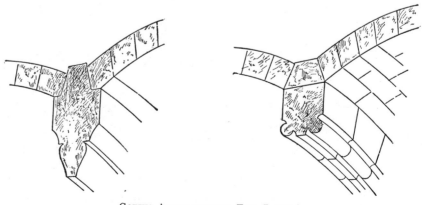

GOTHIC ARCHITECTURE: FIGS. 7 AND 8.

Relation of rib to shell of vault.

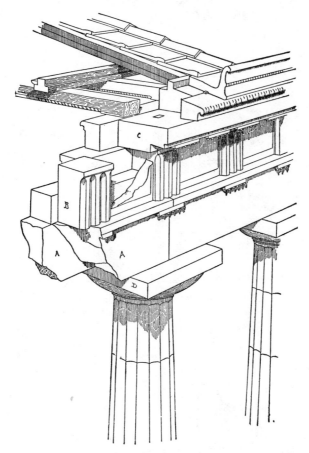

GRECIAN ARCHITECTURE: CONSTRUCTION OF A
DORIC BUILDING.

A, Epistyle or architrave, in this case two stones in depth.
B, Triglyph; the metopes are between the triglyphs, and
this whole horizontal band is the frieze. *C*, Cornice.
D, Abacus of the capital.

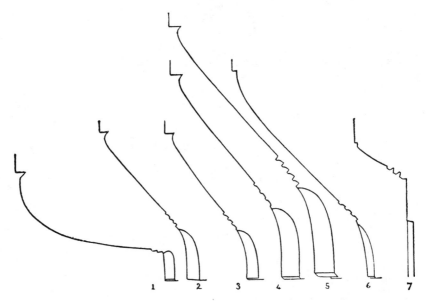

GRECIAN ARCHITECTURE: PROFILES OF DORIC CAPITALS, AS FOLLOWS:

Nos. 1 and 6, early capitals found on the Acropolis at Athens. No. 2, Athens; so-called Temple of Theseus. No. 3, Athens;
Propylaia. Nos. 4 and 5, Athens; Parthenon. No. 7, Cori (Southern Italy); so-called Temple of Hercules.

GRECIAN ARCHITECTURE: ANGLE OF AN IONIC BUILDING; ONE CORNER CAPITAL AND TWO
COMMON IONIC CAPITALS.

The broad band in each capital would be decorated by anthemions in a rich building.

GRECIAN ARCHITECTURE: DETAIL OF AN IONIC BUILDING; NORTH DOORWAY OF ERECHTHEUM, ATHENS.

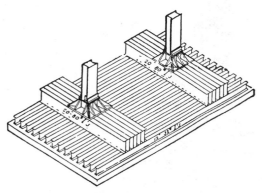

GRILLAGE OF STEEL I BEAMS, WITH TWO IRON
BOX-COLUMNS AND THEIR SHOES.

GROIN: VAULTS WITH GROINS; DORSETSHIRE, C. 1110.

GUTTER: MODERN CHURCH OF S. JEAN-BAPTISTE DE
BELLEVILLE, PARIS.

Metal gutter on stone wall-cornice.

HALF-TIMBERED HOUSE, CALLED NEWGATE, YORK,
ENGLAND, ABOUT 1450.

HALF-TIMBERED HOUSE, MORETON OLD HALL (CHESHIRE), C. 1590.

HALF-TIMBERED (DEFINITION *B*) HOUSE IN HILDES-
HEIM, NEAR HANOVER, GERMANY.

FIG. 1.—HALL OF OAKHAM CASTLE, RUTLANDSHIRE, 12TH CENTURY; INTERIOR.   (SEE FIG. 2.)

FIG. 2.—HALL OF OAKHAM CASTLE. (SEE FIG. 1.)

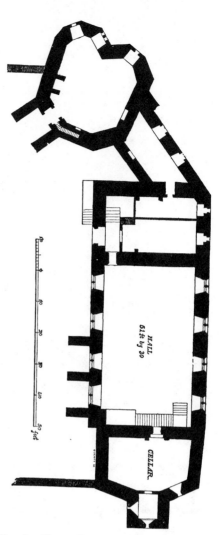

FIG. 3.—HALL: PLAN OF THAT OF STOKESAY CASTLE, SHROPSHIRE. (SEE FIG. 4.)

FIG. 4.—HALL: EXTERIOR OF THAT OF STOKESAY CASTLE, SHROPSHIRE. (SEE FIG. 3.)

FIG. 6. — HALL CALLED SALLE DES MORTS, OURSCAMP, NEAR NOYON (OISE).   (SEE FIG. 5.)

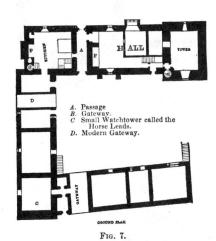

A. Passage
B. Gateway.
C. Small Watchtower called the Horse Leads.
D. Modern Gateway.

FIG. 7.

A. Fireplace.
B.B.B. Lockers.
C.C. Seats in the windows.
D. Drain.

FIG. 8.

FIG. 7. — HALL (DEFINITION *E*): GROUND PLAN OF HOUSE CALLED YANWATH HALL, WESTMORE-LAND.   FIG. 8. — PLAN ON LARGER SCALE OF UPPER STORY OF TOWER IN FIG. 7.

HENRI QUATRE (STYLE OF): FAÇADE, PART OF THE PLACE DAUPHINE, PARIS.

HERRINGBONE
PATTERN.

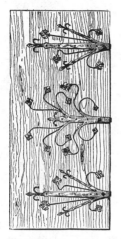

WROUGHT-IRON ORNA-
MENTAL HINGES OF
CHURCH DOOR, SIN-
ZIG.

HINGE: SWISS WROUGHT-
IRON WORK OF SEVEN-
TEENTH CENTURY.

HIP: ROOF WITH FOUR HIPS, NEUKIRCHE, SWITZERLAND, 1734.

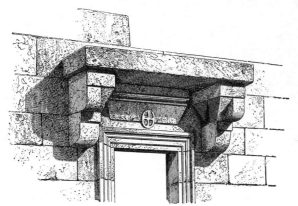

HOOD OVER DOOR; CUT STONE SUPPORTED ON CORBELS; SYRIA, 5TH OR 6TH CENTURY.

HOOD OVER DOOR OF AYRAULT HOUSE, NEWPORT, R.I.

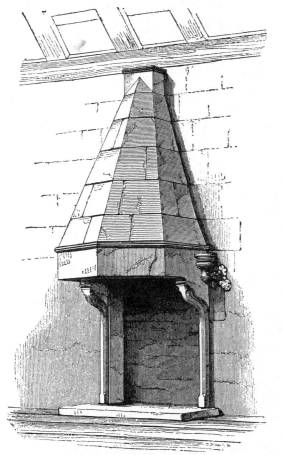

HOOD OVER FIREPLACE IN THE HALL, MEARE, SOMERSETSHIRE.

HOOD OF 12TH CENTURY FIREPLACE, BOOTHBY PAGNEL, LINCOLNSHIRE.

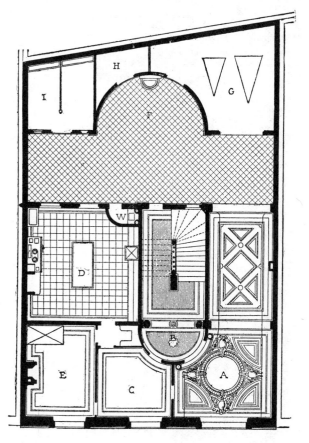

FIG. 1.—HOTEL: PRIVATE HÔTEL, RUE CIMAROSA, PARIS;
PLAN OF REZ-DE-CHAUSSÉE, OR GROUND STORY.

A. Vestibule of *porte cochère* with passage to court.
B. Vestibule to staircase, two steps above A.
C. Porter's room, or office.
D. Kitchen.
E. Bedroom of porter, or office.
F. Court.
G. Carriage house.
H. Harness room.
I. Stable.

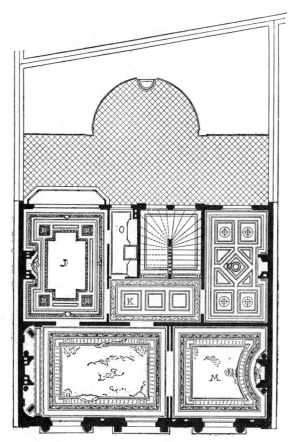

FIG. 2.—HÔTEL: PLAN OF PREMIER ÉTAGE, OR FIRST
STORY ABOVE GROUND STORY. (SEE FIG. 1.)

J. Dining room.
K. Landing place.
L, M. Drawing-rooms (salons).
N. Salon, or library.
O. Service room (butler's pantry).

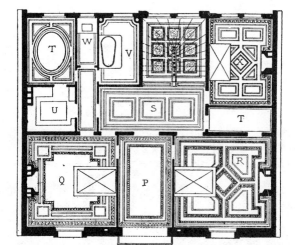

FIG. 3.—HÔTEL: PLAN OF DEUXIÈME ETAGE, OR SECOND STORY ABOVE GROUND STORY. (SEE FIG. 1.)

P. Private sitting room.
Q. Bedroom (mistress of the house).
R. Bedroom (master of the house).
S. Landing place.
T. Dressing room.
U. Closet.
V. Bathroom.
W. W. C.

FIG. 4.—HÔTEL: FAÇADE. (SEE FIGS. 1, 2, 3.)

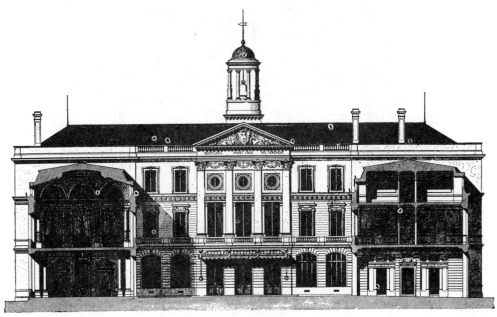

HÔTEL DE VILLE, CAMBRAI (NORD), FRANCE.

HÔTEL DE CLUNY, PARIS.

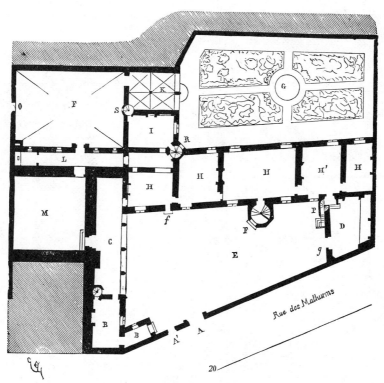

HÔTEL DE CLUNY. PLAN.

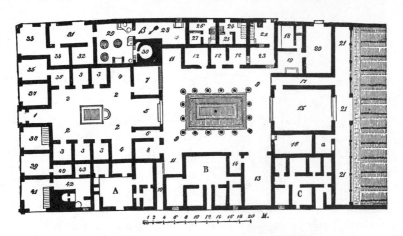

1. Fauces, or entrance passage.
2. Atrium, with impluvium in centre.
3. Cubicula, or of unknown purpose.
4. Alæ of atrium.
5. Tablinum.
6. Andron, sometimes called fauces, leading from atrium to peristyle.
7, 8. Sitting rooms opening on peristyle.
9. Peristyle with large impluvium.
10. Passage leading to posticum (back door).
11. Alæ of peristyle.
12. Cubicula, or unexplained.
13. Probably dining room.
14. Closet.
15. Œcus.
16. Room with floor raised above peristyle, like that of the œcus.
17. Passage leading to garden.
18. Back kitchen or closet.
19. Kitchen.
20. Room leading to street, with separate door, probably for housing a wagon.
21. Colonnade of the garden.
22, 23. Ground floor of separate dwelling with second story.
24, 25, 26, 27. The same.

FIG. 1.—HOUSE: PLAN OF THE INSULA IN POMPEII, CONTAINING THE HOUSE OF PANSA WITH SIX OTHER DWELLINGS AND SEVERAL SHOPS.

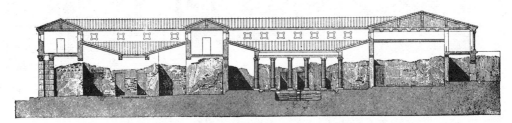

FIG. 2.—HOUSE OF PANSA, POMPEII; LONGITUDINAL SECTION. (SEE PLAN.)

The shaded parts of the drawing show the existing walls; the superstructure being restored from remains of the building found on the site.

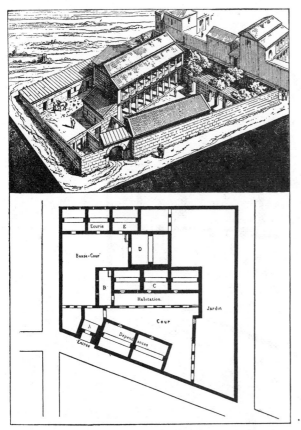

FIG. 3.—HOUSE AT MOUDJELEIA IN SYRIA, OF ROMAN IMPE-
RIAL EPOCH, SHOWING WELL THE ARRANGEMENT OF THE
ROMAN COUNTRY HOUSE IN A QUIET PROVINCE.

FIG. 4.—HOUSE AT S. YRIEIX (HAUTE-VIENNE);
14TH CENTURY.

FIG. 5. — House of 1485, now called Hôtel de Cluny, Paris.

The wall on the right separates the street without from the court, upon which open the doors and stairways of the house, as shown.

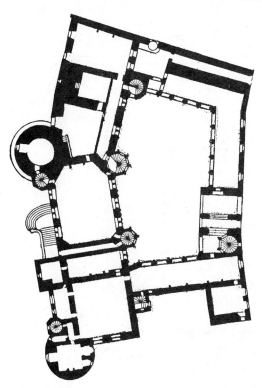

FIG. 6. — House of Jacques Cœur, at Bourges.
PLAN.

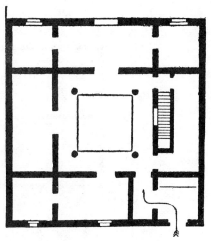

FIG. 7. — House: Typical Plan of Ancient Moorish Dwelling, prepared by C. Uhde for Comparison with Modern Plan. (See Fig. 14.)

FIG. 8.—HOUSE IN BRUGES, C. 1565.

The Gothic forms and details keep their hold on domestic architecture throughout the century.

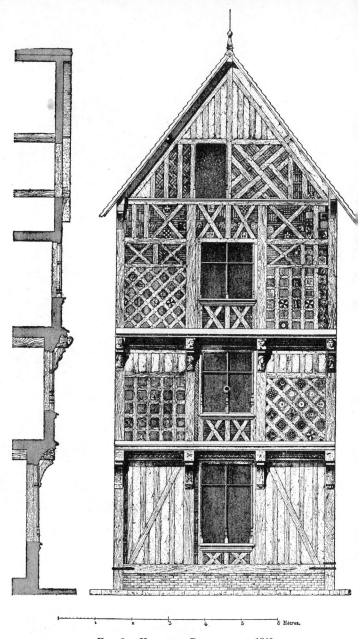

FIG. 9.—HOUSE AT BEAUVAIS, C. 1540.

Good example of the French Renaissance in its simpler manifestations.

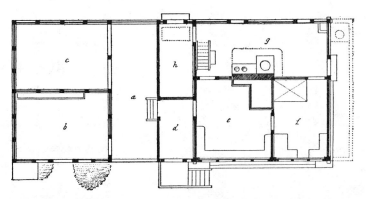

FIG. 10.—HOUSE NEAR FISCHENTHAL, SWITZERLAND; 17TH CENTURY. PLAN. (SEE EXTERIOR.)

a.
b. } Storage for grain and fodder, stable, etc.
c.
d. Vestibule, from which the door on the right leads to the house; that on the left to the barn at *a*, by means of a slight descent.
e. Living room, with great pottery stove in upper right hand corner and fixed bench under the windows.

f. Bedchamber, with fixed bedplace and, near the window, work bench and turning lathe.
g. Kitchen.
h. Store house for wood, with trap door to room above, where provisions, etc., are stored. The arrangement of the story above is very similar, with the addition of the gallery on the right, which in this instance is partly enclosed.

196

FIG. 11.—HOUSE NEAR FISCHENTHAL, SWITZERLAND. (SEE PLAN.)

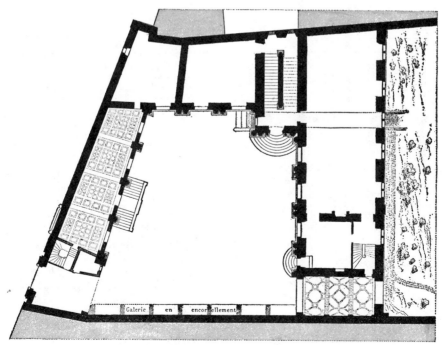

FIG. 12.—HOUSE CALLED HÔTEL D'ASSÉZAT, AT TOULOUSE. PLAN.
See Accouplement, illustration, and Arcade, illustration, for parts of court front.

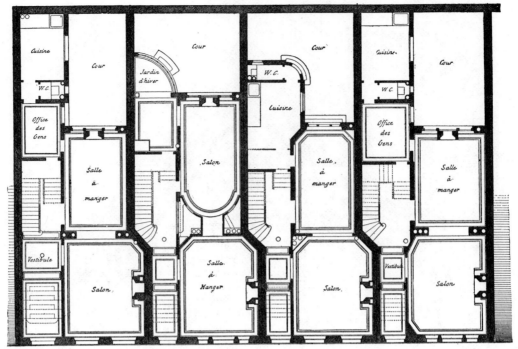

FIG. 13.—ROW OF SMALL HOUSES, RUE D'OFFREMONT, PARIS.
The extreme neatness of the plan is noticeable.

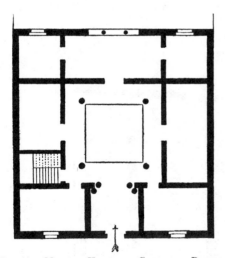

FIG. 14.—MODERN HOUSE AT CORDOVA. PLAN TO
BE COMPARED WITH FIG. 7.
The square court (patio) with four columns is a feature almost
universal in Mediterranean lands at all epochs.

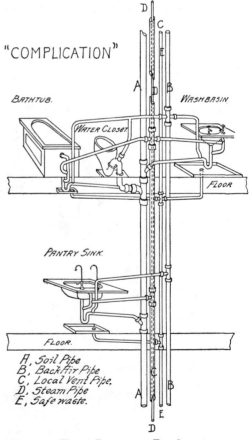

HOUSE DRAINAGE: FIG. 2.

198

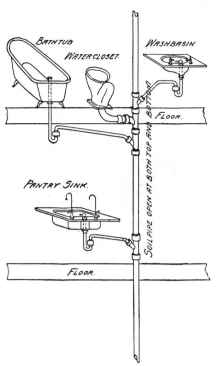

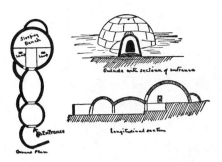

IGLUGEAK: GROUND PLAN; EXTERIOR WITH SEC-
TION OF ENTRANCE; AND LONGITUDINAL SECTION.

HOUSE DRAINAGE: FIG. 3.

INLAY: BLACK AND WHITE MARBLE; PAVEMENT
OF BAPTISTERY, FLORENCE; C. 1200.

INLAY: BLACK AND WHITE MARBLE; PAVEMENT, CHURCH
OF S. MINIATO, NEAR FLORENCE; C. 1350.

199

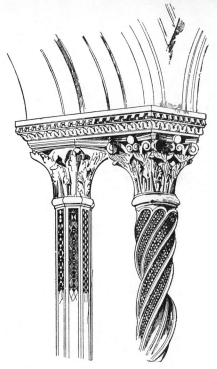

INLAY WITH GLASS TESSERAL (COSMATI
WORK) SHAFTS OF COLUMNS; CLOIS-
TERS OF S. JOHN LATERAN, ROME.

INLAY: SWISS; 17TH CENTURY.

INTERLACE: INTERLACED PATTERNS FROM THE ALHAMBRA, GRANADA, SPAIN.

INTERLACE: INTERLACED
ORNAMENT, CANTER-
BURY CATHEDRAL;
CRYPT.

INTERLACE: INTERLACING ARCHIVOLT, CANTER-
BURY CATHEDRAL; c. 1120.

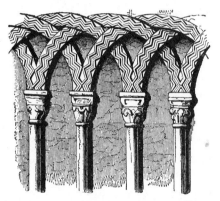

INTERLACE: INTERLACING ARCHIVOLT, CHURCH OF
S. JOHN, DEVIZES; c. 1160.

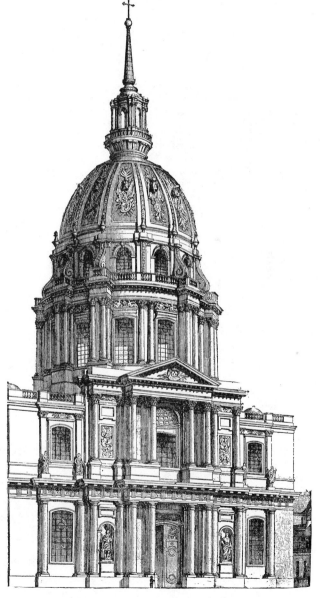

INVALIDES: THE LATER CHURCH, CALLED DÔME DES INVALIDES;
BUILT 1706.

IONIC CAPITAL LYING ON THE ACROPOLIS, ATHENS.

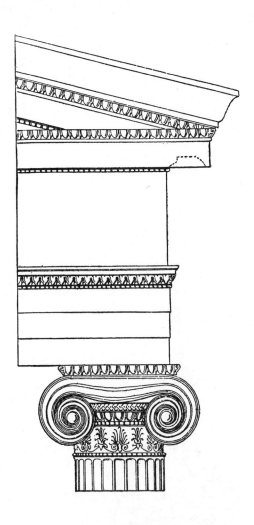

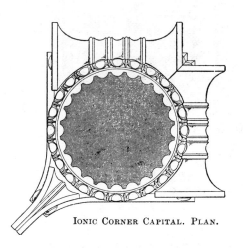

IONIC CORNER CAPITAL. PLAN.

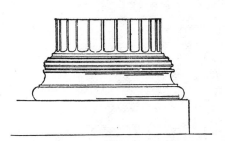

ORDER OF THE ERECHTHEUM, ATHENS, GREECE.

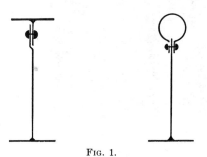

FIG. 1.

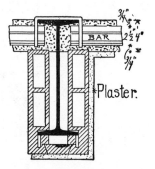

IRON CONSTRUCTION: FLOOR
OF CONCRETE AND IRON
BARS HUNG FROM I BEAMS,
THESE BEING PROTECTED
FROM FIRE BY TERRA-
COTTA CASING.

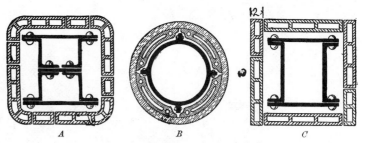

IRON CONSTRUCTION: THREE FORMS OF COLUMNS ENCLOSED BY FIRE-
PROOFING OF TERRA-COTTA BLOCKS.

A, Z-bar column; B, a special form composed of four quadrantal bars of iron;
C, channel-beam column.

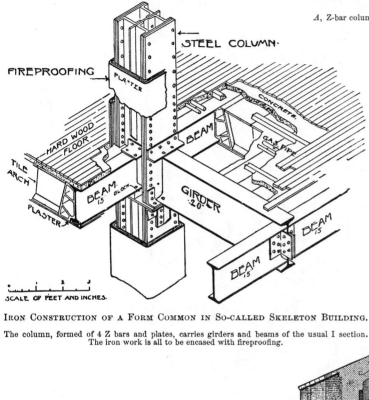

IRON CONSTRUCTION OF A FORM COMMON IN SO-CALLED SKELETON BUILDING.

The column, formed of 4 Z bars and plates, carries girders and beams of the usual I section.
The iron work is all to be encased with fireproofing.

ITALY, PART III.—LOMBARDY: CHURCH OF S. AMBRO-
GIO, MILAN. PART OF CROSS SECTION THROUGH NAVE
AND AISLE; 11TH AND 12TH CENTURIES.

ITALY, PART III. — LOMBARDY: CHURCH OF S. MICHELE, PAVIA. ONE BAY OF NAVE; 11TH AND 12TH CENTURIES.

ITALY, PART IV. — VENETIA: CHURCH OF S. FOSCA, TORCELLO; EAST END.

ITALY, PART IV. — VENETIA: CHURCH OF THE FRARI,
(S. MARIA GLORIOSA DEI FRARI), VENICE.

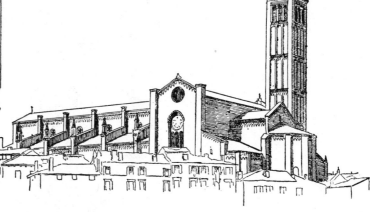

ITALY, PART IV. — VENETIA: CHURCH OF S. ANASTASIA, VERONA; 13TH CENTURY; CAMPANILE OF
15TH CENTURY.

ITALY, PART IV. — VENETIA: CHURCH OF S. FERMO,
VERONA.

ITALY, PART IV. — VENETIA: TWO WINDOWS OF
TYPICALLY VENETIAN FORM.

ITALY, PART IV.—VENETIA: AISLE WINDOW,
S. ANASTASIA, VERONA.

ITALY, PART VII.—TUSCANY: NAVE OF S. M. NOVELLA, FLORENCE.

ITALY, PART VII.—TUSCANY: NAVE OF CATHEDRAL OF FLORENCE.

206

ITALY, PART IX. — LATIUM OR LAZIO: RESTORED VIEW OF TEMPLE AT CORA; ABOUT 80 B.C.

This building is unique in style, a modified Grecian Doric of singular delicacy. See profile of capital under Grecian Architecture, and doorway below.

ITALY, PART IX. — LATIUM: DOOR IN THE TEMPLE OF HERCULES AT CORA.

207

ITALY, PART X.—ABRUZZI: CHURCH AT SANTA MARIA D' ARBONA, NEAR THE ADRIATIC; C. 1210 A.D.

JACOBEAN MANOR HOUSE, BRAMSHILL (SURREY);
1609 A.D.

JOGGLE : HOOD OVER FIREPLACE, THE LINTEL
BUILT OF STONES MUTUALLY SUPPORTING ONE
ANOTHER BY JOGGLES ; 14TH CENTURY ; EDLING-
HAM CASTLE, NORTHUMBERLAND.

KERAMICS IN ARCHITECTURE: CLOISTER OF SAN
STEFANO, BOLOGNA.

The arches and the superstructure of brick of two colours, cast
to shape, and of small tiles.

KELTIC : CROSS OF MUREDACH, MONASTERBOICE,
IRELAND, OF THE TYPE KNOWN AS KELTIC
CROSS, AND BEARING KELTIC DECORATIVE
SCULPTURE.

KEY (IN SENSE B) : WEDGES OR PINS HOLDING IN
PLACE THE FRAMING OF A SWISS TIMBER HOUSE.

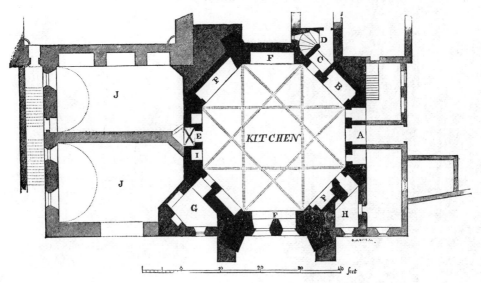

KITCHEN OF THE ANCIENT MONASTERY, DURHAM, ENGLAND; 14TH CENTURY.

A. Entrance.
B. Chimney for smoking meat, etc.
C. Passage to deanery.
D. Stair to roof.
E. Doorway, now closed.

F F. Fireplaces.
G. Scullery.
H. Storeroom.
I. Cistern.
J. Buildings, now removed.

The room is vaulted by means of intersecting ribs which support a flat roof, surrounded by a battlemented parapet.

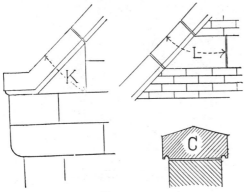

KNEELER.

C. The stone coping of a gable shown in section.
K. Kneeler at spring of gable.
L. Kneeler at high level, preventing too great a pressure diagonally upon K.

KNOCKER OF BRONZE, FROM A PALAZZO AT BOLOGNA; 16TH CENTURY.

LABEL: DOORWAY, CLOISTER OF S. GREGORIO,
VALLADOLID, SPAIN.

(Compare cut under Doorway, viz., that of Coombe Church;
and under Dripstone.)

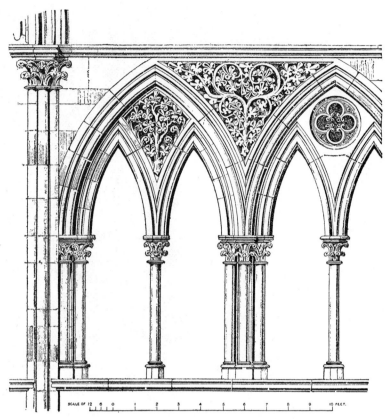

LANCET: TRIFORIUM OF CHOIR, LE MANS CATHEDRAL.

Two lancet arches beneath an equilateral arch, the concentricity of the arcs showing how the lancet
is an arch whose two centres are brought near together.

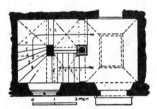

LANDING: FIG. 1.

The arrow above points up-stairs, and the figures denote the
risers; 1, 2, 3, fliers, 5, 6, etc., winders. The arrow below
points down stairs, and 1 is the top riser of the lower flight.
(See the view, Fig. 2.)

LANDING: FIG. 2. (SEE FIG. 1.)

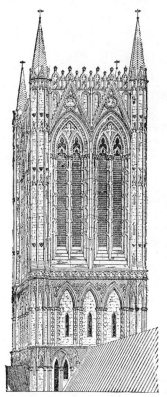

LANTERN (DEFINITION *A*): CENTRAL TOWER,
LINCOLN CATHEDRAL.

LANTERN (DEFINITION *B*) OF CUT STONE, WITH
WICKET OF WROUGHT IRON; CHÂTEAUDUN
(EURE-ET-LOIR), FRANCE.

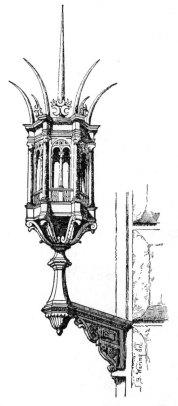

LANTERN (DEFINITION *B*) OF BRONZE; EXTERIOR
OF PALAZZO STROZZI, FLORENCE.

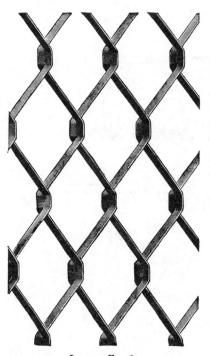

LATH: FIG. 1.

Metallic Lath, made of sheet metal cut and bent so as to
produce a fabric with meshes not unlike woven wire.

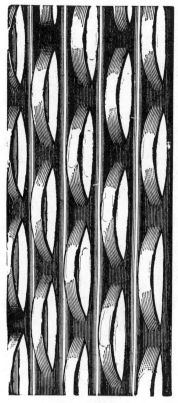

LATH: FIG. 2.

Metallic Lath, made of sheet metal cut and corrugated, and
the curved parts forced into projection.

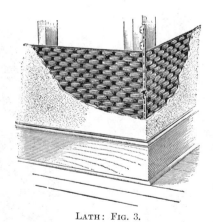

LATH: FIG. 3.

The metallic Lath, Fig. 2, shown in place, with steel corner
strip.

LAVATORY IN THE CLOISTER OF THE CHURCH OF
S. ALEXIS, ROME.

The decoration in mosaic is of the general character of Cosmati
work.

LAVATORY IN THE ABBEY OF S. DENIS; NOW IN THE ÉCOLE DES BEAUX ARTS, PARIS.
The water spirted from the spouts between the heads.

LECTERN OF BRASS, CHURCH OF NOTRE DAME, AACHEN (AIX-LA-CHAPELLE), RHENISH PRUSSIA.
Fig. 1, plan; Fig. 2, large scale detail of one corner of triangular centrepiece; Fig. 3, large scale detail of one of the buttress towers.

LECTERN, AT ANGLE OF MARBLE PULPIT, CHURCH OF S. BARTOLOMEO, PISTOJA, TUSCANY; c. 1520.

214

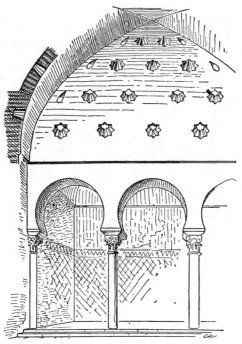

LIGHTING OF A BATH IN THE ALHAMBRA BY STAR-
SHAPED OPENINGS IN THE VAULT; SEE SECTION
AT LEFT.

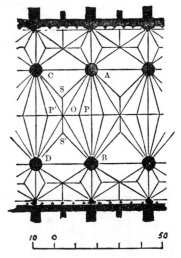

10   0   50

LIERNE RIB: PLAN OF VAULTING; NAVE OF
LINCOLN CATHEDRAL.

LINTELS CUT TO THE
SEMBLANCE OF A
CONSTRUCTIVE
ARCH; KHERBET-
HÂSS, SYRIA.

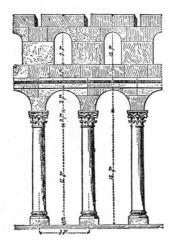

LINTELS IN NAVE OF BASILICA AT MOUDJELEIA,
SYRIA.

LIVING ROOM IN WEALTHY PEASANT'S HOUSE, FRANCE.

Permanent or standing bed-places; chimney breast and mantel carried on corbels: a modern design.

LOGGIA: FIG. 1. — HOUSE AT REFADE, SYRIA; 6TH CENTURY.

Front on court, with loggia in upper story.

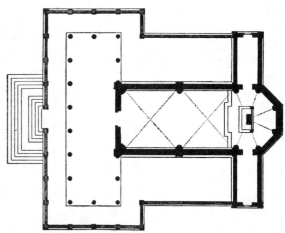

LOGGIA: FIG. 2. — CHURCH OF S. MARIA DELLE GRAZIE, NEAR AREZZO, TUSCANY.

With loggia much wider than façade of church. The outer wall has been removed.

LOGGIA DEI LANZI, FLORENCE.

The interior without the statues and groups; the Palazzio Vecchio beyond.

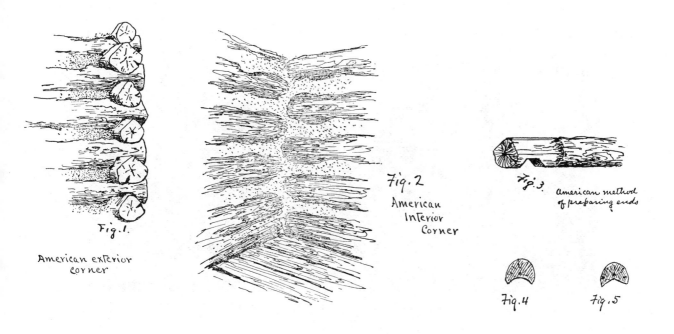

Fig. 1.

American exterior
corner

Fig. 2
American
Interior
Corner

Fig. 3.

american method
of preparing ends

Fig. 4   Fig. 5

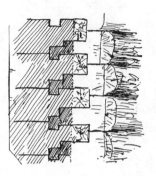

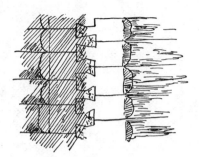

Fig. 6.

Fig. 7

Section on line of partition
Russian method.

Fig. 8. Russian outside corner
with ends cut off.

Fig. 9.
Russian method of
preparing ends.
a dressed log.

LOG HOUSE: FIG. 10.—THAT BUILT FOR THE RUSSIAN EXHIBITION AT VIENNA IN 1873.

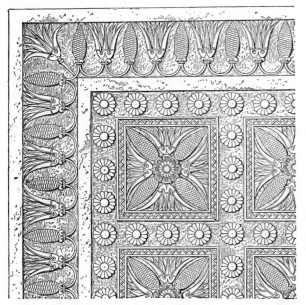

THE LOTUS IN SCULPTURE: THE OUTSIDE BORDER SHOWING ALTERNATELY THE BUD AND THE DEVELOPED FLOWER; THE SAME UNITS OF DECORATION USED IN THE PANELS. ASSYRIAN SCULPTURE FROM KOUYUNJIK.

LOUIS XIV. ARCHITECTURE: FIG. 1.— INTERIOR OF CHAPEL, CHÂTEAU AT VERSAILLES.

LOUIS XV. ARCHITECTURE: FIG. 3. — PAVILION, HÔTEL
SOUBISE, PARIS; c. 1730.

See interior of upper story below.

LOUIS XV. ARCHITECTURE: FIG. 4. — INTERIOR OF PAVILION, HÔTEL SOUBISE, PARIS; c. 1730.

See exterior, Fig. 3.

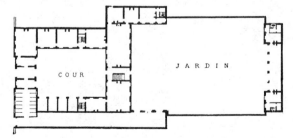

LOUIS XIII. ARCHITECTURE: FIG. 1. — PLAN OF HÔTEL DE SULLY, PARIS, RUE ST. ANTOINE.

Wheeled vehicles can enter the court (cour), and also the broad alley which leads to the garden (jardin). Stables are on the right
as one enters the court.

LOUIS XIII. ARCHITECTURE: FIG. 3. — PORTE-COCHÈRE RUE DES
FRANCS-BOURGEOIS, PARIS.

LOUIS XIII. ARCHITECTURE: FIG. 4. — CHURCH OF S. PAUL
S. LOUIS, PARIS; 1627.

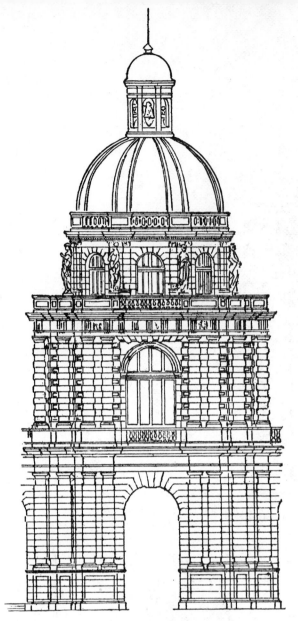

LUXEMBOURG, PALACE OF THE, PARIS: PAVILION OF
ENTRANCE; C. 1620 A.D.

MACHICOLATION: A
SIMPLE FORM;
13TH OR 14TH CEN-
TURY.

The parapet wall, about
20 inches thick, rests
upon a row of corbels,
with an open space
about 12 inches wide
between the parapet
and the face of the
rampart.

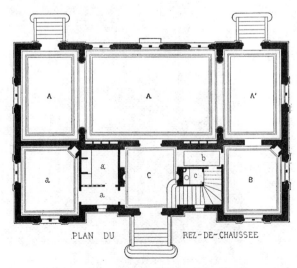

PLAN DU REZ-DE-CHAUSSEE

MAIRIE DE L'ISLE-ADAM (SEINE-ET-OISE). PLAN.

A, A. Halls for meetings and festivities, one of them serving for marriages; the large room covered by a flat terrace roof (see
exterior below).   *A'*. Room for municipal council.   *B*. Office of secretary.   *C*. Vestibule.   *a, a*. Residence of janitor.
b. Passage.   *c*. Toilet.

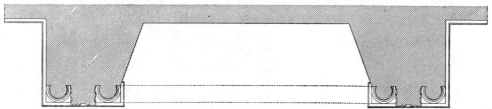

MANTELPIECE IN THE HÔTEL DE CLARY, TOULOUSE (HAUTE GARONNÉ); DATE ABOUT 1575.
Of peculiar local style.

MASONRY OF RUBBLE BEDDED IN MORTAR, FACED
WITH SQUARED RUBBLE AND HAVING BOND
COURSES OF THIN BRICKS.

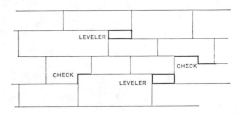

MASONRY: CUT TO ILLUSTRATE FACING OF STONE
WALL.

MEGALITHIC MONUMENT: CROMLECH NEAR SAUMUR (MAINE-ET-LOIRE), FRANCE.

MEGALITHIC MONUMENT: MENHIR AT GRABUSSON
(ILE ET VILAINE, FRANCE).

MEGALITHIC MONUMENT AT CARNAC (MORBIHAN),
FRANCE.
The cross is comparatively recent.

BRIDGE WITH MEMORIAL ARCHES AT SAINT-CHAMAS (BOUCHES DU RHÔNE), FRANCE.

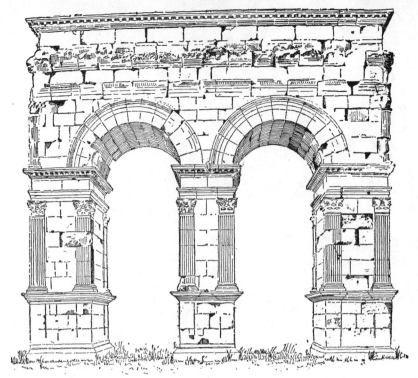

MEMORIAL ARCH AT SAINTES (CHARENTE INFÉRIEURE), FRANCE.

It has been removed piece by piece and rebuilt.

MEMORIAL ARCH IN THE FORUM, ROME, DEDICATED TO SEPTIMIUS SEVERUS.

MEMORIAL COLUMN, NEAR S. MARIA NOVELLA, FLORENCE.

The work of Giovanni Pisano; erected 1308, in memory of a theological movement. The capital shows emblems of the four evangelists.

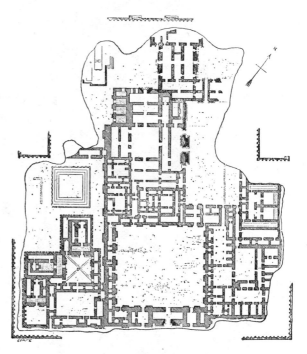

MESOPOTAMIA: PLAN OF THE PALACE OF SARGON.

MESOPOTAMIA: CONJECTURAL RESTORATION (CHIPIEZ AFTER STRABO) OF A GREAT TEMPLE SUCH AS THAT CALLED "THE OBSERVATORY" AT KHORSABAD.

METAL WORK: BRONZE PARAPET OF STAIRS; HOTEL DEMIDOFF, PARIS.

METAL WORK: WROUGHT-IRON HINGES AND LOCKS, 13TH CENTURY; ARMOIRE IN CATHEDRAL OF BAYEUX, NORMANDY.

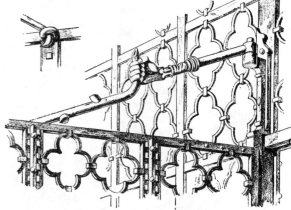

METAL WORK: WROUGHT-IRON TENSION-ROD AND HINGE FROM GATE; ORVIETO CATHEDRAL.

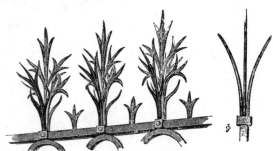

METAL WORK: SHEET- AND WROUGHT-IRON; CREST OF METAL RAILING, VERONA.

METAL WORK: MODERN; CAST AND MACHINE-WROUGHT: GRENELLE MARKET, PARIS. (SEE COL. 890.)

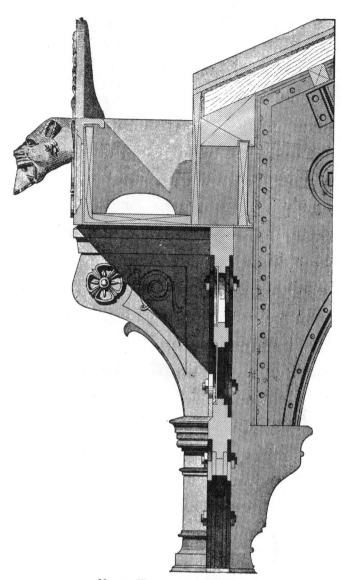

METAL WORK: MODERN; CAST AND MACHINE-WROUGHT; GRENELLE MARKET, PARIS. (SEE COL. 887.)

METAL WORK: WROUGHT-IRON GUARD FOR FANLIGHT; HOTEL, RUE S. PAUL, PARIS.

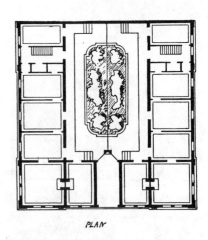

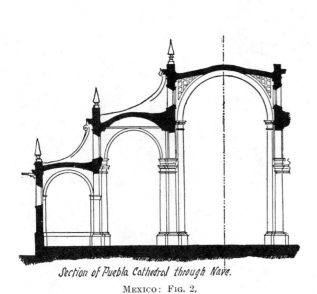

Section of Puebla Cathedral through Nave.

MEXICO: FIG. 2,

PLAN

SECTION

House. Mexico City. DWELLING FOR 2 FAMILIES

MEXICO: FIG. 3.

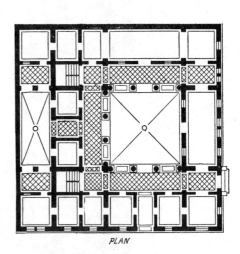

PLAN

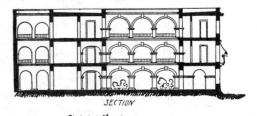

SECTION

Hotel. Monterey.

MEXICO: FIG. 5.

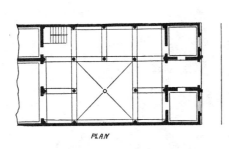

PLAN

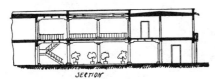

SECTION

House Guadalajara

MEXICO: FIG. 4.

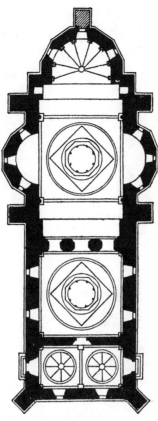

MOLDAVIA, ARCHITECTURE OF :
FIG. 1.—CHURCH AT JASSY,
CALLED BISERICA TREI ERARHI.
PLAN.

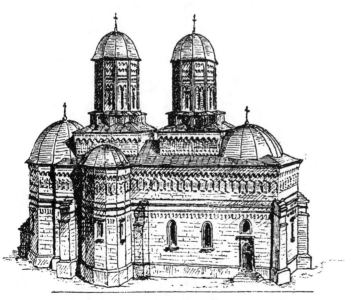

MOLDAVIA, ARCHITECTURE OF: FIG. 2.—BISERICA TREI ERARHI
IN JASSY. (SEE FIG. 1.)

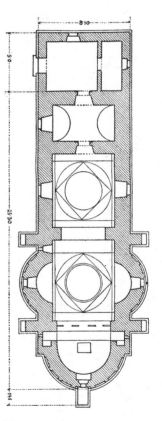

MOLDAVIA, ARCHITECTURE OF:
FIG. 3.—CHURCH AT BUR-
DUSCHENY (BURDUSENI).
PLAN.

231

MONASTIC ARCHITECTURE: REFECTORY AT FOSSANOVA. (SEE CHAPTER HOUSE, ABOVE.)

MONOGRAM FROM A NECROPOLIS AT EL-BARAH, SYRIA.

X P for Christos, with alpha (to right) and omega.

MONUMENT AT S. REMY (BOUCHES DU RHÔNE); PROBABLY OF THE 3D CENTURY, A.D.

MONASTIC ARCHITECTURE: VIEW OF MONASTERY OF MAULBRONN. (SEE PLAN ABOVE.)

MONASTIC ARCHITECTURE: CHAPTER HOUSE AT FOSSANOVA, LATIUM, ITALY.

MOLDAVIA, ARCHITECTURE OF: FIG. 4.—CHURCH AT BURDUS-
CHENY (BURDUSENI). (SEE FIG. 3.)

MOLDAVIA, ARCHITECTURE OF: FIG. 5. — WOODEN CHURCH AT KLOKUCZKA.

MOLDAVIA, ARCHITECTURE OF: FIG. 6. — WINDOW
IN CHURCH AT RADAUTZ, SHOWING STRONG
WESTERN INFLUENCE, AS OF THE 15TH CENTURY
GOTHIC OF GERMANY.

MONASTIC ARCHITECTURE: BUILDINGS OF THE MONASTERY AT CLUNY;
ROMANESQUE TOWER OF SOUTH TRANSEPT.

MOORISH ARCHITECTURE: BRICK ARCADE ON EX-
TERIOR OF THE GIRALDA, SEVILLE, SPAIN.

MOORISH ARCHITECTURE: DOORWAY, TARRAGONA,
SPAIN.

MOORISH ARCHITECTURE: VERY EARLY STYLE;
MOSQUE, CORDOVA, SPAIN.

MOORISH ARCHITECTURE:
SCROLL PATTERN FROM
THE ALHAMBRA.

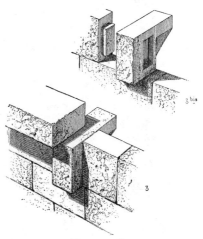

MORTISE PUT TO UNUSUAL SERVICE: TO HOLD A
CORBEL FIRMLY IN PLACE IN SOLID CUT-STONE
MASONRY; SYRIA, 5TH CENTURY, A.D.

235

MOSAIC FLOOR: MONASTERY CHURCH AT ARN-
STEIN, RHENISH PRUSSIA.

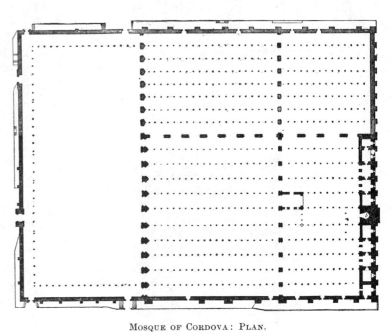

MOSQUE OF CORDOVA: PLAN.

On the left is the open court.   (See interior view below, and exterior under Moorish Architecture.)

MOSQUE OF CORDOVA: INTERIOR VIEW.

(See plan above.)

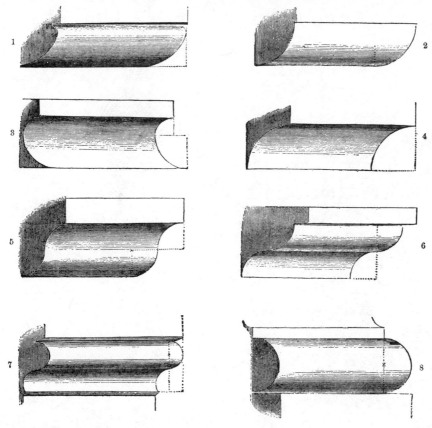

MOULDING:

1. Ovolo moulding from the Doric Temple, Corinth.
2. Ovolo moulding from the Theatre of Marcellus, Rome.
3. Scotia, or Trochilus, Baths of Diocletian, Rome.
4. Cavetto.

5. Cyma Recta.
6. Cyma Reversa.   (5 and 6 are forms of the Ogee.)
7. Ogee of late Roman work.
8. Torus, from Palladio's works.

MOULDING: 12TH CENTURY: FROM S. EBBE'S CHURCH, OXFORDSHIRE, AND FROM LINCOLN CATHEDRAL.

MOULDING: VENETIAN; 14TH CENTURY; A VARIETY OF DENTIL MOULDING.

MOULDING: 12TH CENTURY: CHURCH OF SAINT CROSS, HANTS.

MOULDING: VENETIAN; WITH GEOMETRICAL FIGURES IN RELIEF.

MOULDING: HOOD-MOULD-
ING OF WINDOW, FROM
WITNEY, OXON.

MUDEJAR ARCHITECTURE:
HOUSE AT SEVILLE, BE-
GUN ABOUT 1500.

MULLION IN FORM OF A FREE COLUMN; HOUSE
OF THE 6TH CENTURY, REFADI, SYRIA.

MULLION: CATHEDRAL AT PISA, TUSCANY, IN FORM OF A FREE
COLUMN, CARRYING SUBORDINATE ARCHES.

MURAL PAINTING, POMPEII: CEILING OF BATHS NEAR THE PORTE STABIANA.

239

MURAL PAINTING: UPPER CHURCH OF S. FRANCIS AT ASSISI, ITALY.

MURAL PAINTING: 12TH AND 13TH CENTURIES; CHURCH
OF S. FRANCIS ASSISI; SECTION SHOWING ONE BAY
OF UPPER AND OF LOWER CHURCH.

MURAL PAINTING: 14TH CENTURY; ONE BAY OF NAVE
OF S. ANASTASIA AT VERONA.

MURAL PAINTING: PART OF TRIFORIUM OF NAVE OF
S. FRANCESCO AT ASSISI.

NECROPOLIS AT MYRA IN LYCIA, ASIA MINOR: TOMBS
CUT IN THE CLIFF OF SOFT STONE.

NEOCLASSIC: EARLIEST FORM, ITALIAN RENAISSANCE; CHURCH OF S. FANTINO, VENICE.

NEOCLASSIC OF THE ITALIAN CINQUE CENTO: CHURCH OF
THE REDEEMER AT VENICE, ITALY.

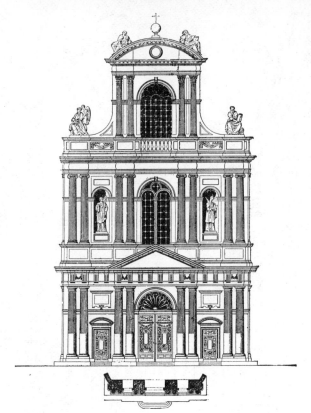

NEOCLASSIC OF THE STYLE LOUIS TREIZE; CHURCH
OF S. GERVAIS AND S. PROTAIS, PARIS.

NEOCLASSIC OF THE ITALIAN CLASSICISMO: COLONNADE IN PIAZZA OF S. PIETRO, ROME; BEGUN 1667.

NEWEL OF STAIRCASE, HOSPITAL DE LA CRUZ, TO-
LEDO, SPAIN; EARLY YEARS OF 16TH CENTURY.

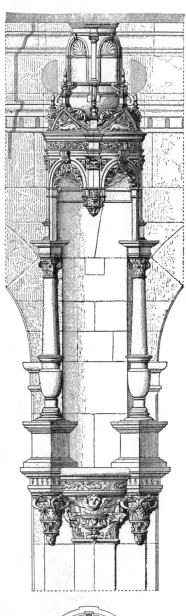

NICHE OF THE GRAND STAIRCASE, CHÂTEAU OF
CHAMBORD; WORK OF THE FRENCH RENAIS-
SANCE; TIME OF FRANCIS I.

NEWEL SERVING AS A PILLAR TO CARRY A VAULTED
ROOF; ÖESTERLÄNGATAN, 17TH CENTURY.

NICHE: ONE ON THE LEFT FOR A PISCINA.

The three openings of the sedilia are also called niches, by an
easy extension of the meaning.

NORTH AFRICA: ROMAN PRÆTORIUM OF 2D CENTURY A.D., AT LAMBESE, ALGERIA.

NOTCH ORNAMENT IN WOOD: THE PLANKSHEER
OF A VENETIAN BOAT.

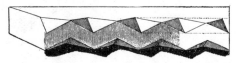

NOTCH ORNAMENT: A MARBLE MOULDING FROM
TOMB OF DOGE ANDREA DANDOLO, S. MARK'S
CHURCH, VENICE.

246

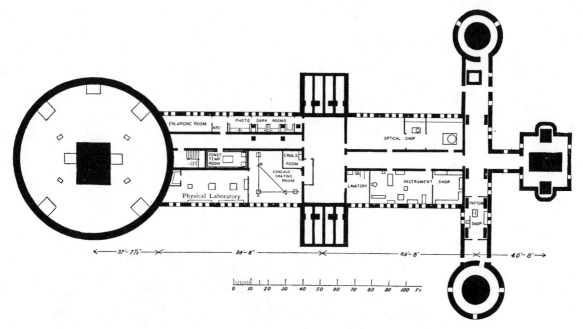

OBSERVATORY AT WILLIAMS BAY (SEE NEXT FIGURE); GROUND FLOOR.

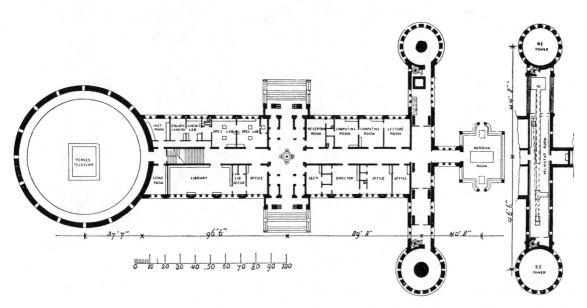

OBSERVATORY AT WILLIAMS BAY, WISCONSIN, BELONGING TO THE UNIVERSITY OF CHICAGO; PRINCIPAL FLOOR: AND UPPER FLOOR OF EASTERN TOWERS.

ORDER, Fig. 1: Grecian Doric; that of the so-called Temple of Neptune at Pæstum.

ORDER: GRECIAN DORIC; THAT OF THE PARTHENON: HAVING THE ENTABLATURE MUCH LESS HIGH AND
THE ECHINUS MUCH LESS SPREADING, IN PROPORTION, THAN THOSE AT PAESTUM.

ORDER, IN SENSE *A*: LOWER ARCHES OF TWO ORDERS, THE UPPER
ORDER HEAVILY MOULDED; UPPER ARCHES OF THREE ORDERS;
THE GREAT ARCHES CARRYING THE TOWER OF TWO ORDERS;
JEDBURGH ABBEY, SCOTLAND.

ORDER, IN SENSE *A*: ARCH OF
TWO ORDERS, EACH HAVING ITS
CARVED HOOD MOULDING, THE
VOUSSOIRS OF THE SUPERIOR
ORDER OF TWO COLOURS. PISA
CATHEDRAL.

ORIEL AT EAST END OF THE CHAPEL, PRUDHOE CASTLE,
NORTHUMBERLAND. PLAN.

ORIEL: SEE THE PLAN, ABOVE.

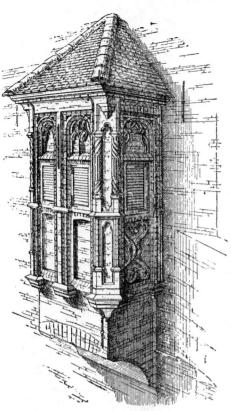

ORIEL, FRONT OF A HOUSE IN BRUGES; C. 1515.

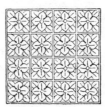

ORNAMENT IN LOW
RELIEF. GOTHIC
SCULPTURE.

ORNAMENT: ENGLISH ROMANESQUE SCULPTURE;
THE SPACES OF AN ARCADE FILLED ALTERNATELY
WITH A FIGURE AND A PANEL OF SCROLL-WORK.

ORNAMENT CARVED IN RELIEF; BETOURSA, SYRIA;
5TH CENTURY.

OVERDOOR PANEL; MODERN PARISIAN WORK, IN LOUIS XIV.
STYLE.

OVERDOOR PANELLING AND FRONTON, FORMING AN
ATTIC; 16TH CENTURY; TORPA, SWEDEN.

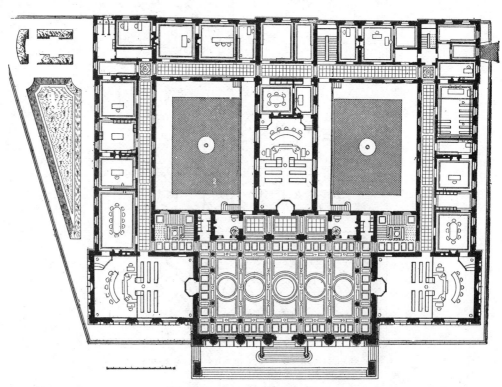

PALAIS DE JUSTICE, HÂVRE. PLAN.
Three court rooms open out of the great vestibule of entrance.   The corridors are lighted from the great courts.

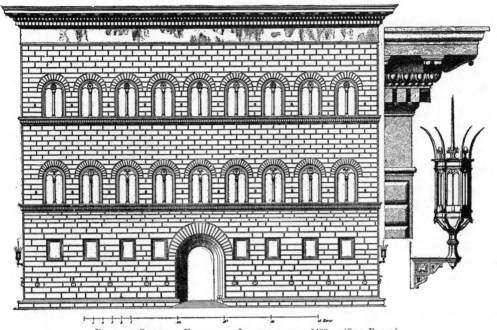

PALAZZO STROZZI, FLORENCE, ITALY; ABOUT 1489. (SEE PLAN.)
The cornicione and one of the lanterns are given on the right.

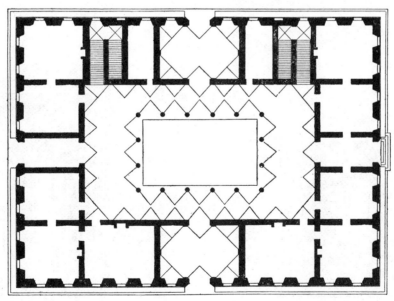

PALAZZO: PLAN OF THE PALAZZO STROZZI, FLORENCE.

PALLADIAN ARCHITECTURE: PALAZZO TIENE AT VICENZA; ABOUT 1556.

PANEL WITH CARVED DIAPER, AND SECONDARY OR
INNER PANEL WITH GOTHIC TRACERY; C. 1500.

PANEL WITH HERALDIC ESCUTCHEON: MONUMENT
OF JOHN LANGSTON CAVERSFIELD, BUCKING-
HAMSHIRE, A.D. 1487.

PANEL: LATE TUDOR TRACERY WITH CARVED
HERALDIC BEARINGS OR COGNIZANCES; LAYER
MARNEY HALL; C. 1530.

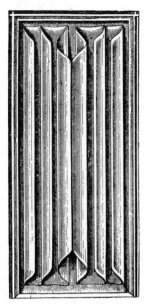

LINEN PANEL; LAYER MARNEY HALL, ESSEX,
ENGLAND; CIRCA 1530.

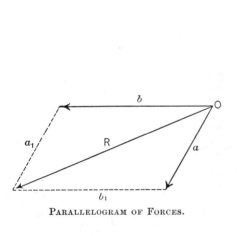

PARALLELOGRAM OF FORCES.

THE PANTHEON, ROME.

Isabelle's restoration, which, however, omits the bronze shutter of the oculus.

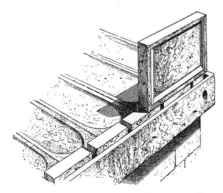

PARAPET OF SOLID SLABS, WITH ROOF AND GUTTER
ALL OF CUT STONE; SYRIA; 5TH CENTURY A.D.

PARAPET WITH PIECED TREFOILS: S. MARY'S
CHURCH, OXFORD; C. 1280.

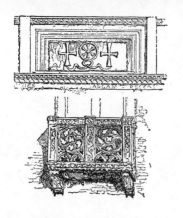

PARAPET WITH PIERCED TRACERY; S. MARY
MAGDALENE, OXFORD; A.D. 1337.

PARAPET: THREE VENETIAN PATTERNS, COMMON
IN BALCONIES:

No. 1. Byzantine style, 11th century.
No. 2. Florid Gothic, late 14th century.
No. 3. 14th or 15th century, with baluster columns.

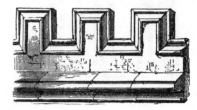

PARAPET CUT INTO SMALL CRENELLATIONS IMI-
TATING BATTLEMENTS; S. PETER'S CHURCH,
DORCHESTER, ENGLAND; c. 1450.

PARAPET, CATHEDRAL OF SANTIAGO DE COMPOSTELLA, SPAIN; 1520 TO 1540.

PARAPET, CATHEDRAL OF SEVILLE, SPAIN; 17TH CENTURY.

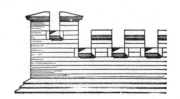

PARAPET: MODERN PATTERNS IN BRICKWORK, WHICH MUST BE CAREFULLY LAID IN STRONG
CEMENT MORTAR.

PARGETTING, DATED 1642, BUT PRESERVING ELIZA-
BETHAN MOTIVE; HIGH STREET, OXFORD.

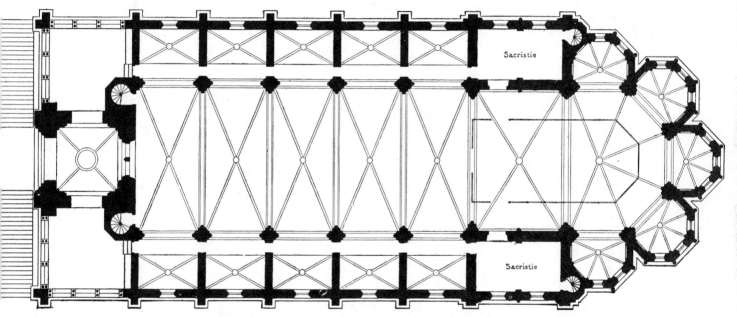

PASSAGE AISLE, CHAPEL OF NOTRE DAME DE LOURDES (HAUTES-PYRÉNÉES).
The aisle is separately roofed, between the nave pillars and the buttress walls which separate the chapels.

PATENT HAMMER.

PELE TOWER, ON THE ENGLISH AND SCOTTISH BORDER: AYDON
HALL, NORTHUMBERLAND.
The undefended doorways opened into the base-court, of which the high wall is
now destroyed.

PENDANT: WINDOW HEAD CUT INTO RESEMBLANCE OF TWO ARCHES, WITH PENDANT INSTEAD OF MULLION.

PENDANT OF FAN VAULTING; HENRY THE SEVENTH'S CHAPEL, WESTMINSTER; A.D. 1510.

PENDANT, 17TH CENTURY, AT SCHLOSS KALMAR, SWEDEN.

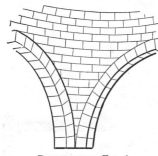

PENDENTIVE, FIG. 1.

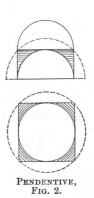

PENDENTIVE, FIG. 2.

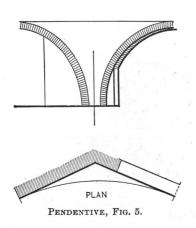

PLAN

PENDENTIVE, FIG. 5.

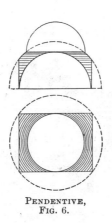

PENDENTIVE, FIG. 6.

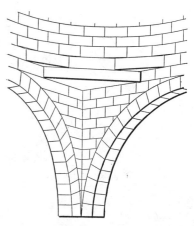

PENDENTIVE, FIG. 8.

258

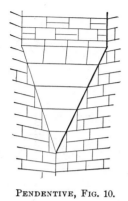

PENDENTIVE, FIG. 10.

PENDENTIVE, FIG. 11.

PLAN

PENDENTIVE, FIG. 12.

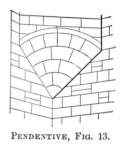

PENDENTIVE, FIG. 13.

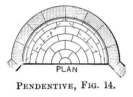

PLAN

PENDENTIVE, FIG. 14.

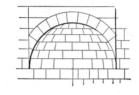

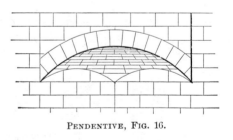

PENDENTIVE, FIG. 16.

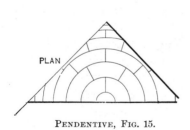

PLAN

PENDENTIVE, FIG. 15.

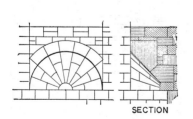

SECTION

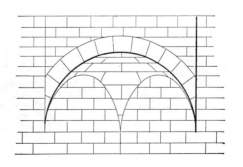

PENDENTIVE, FIG. 19.

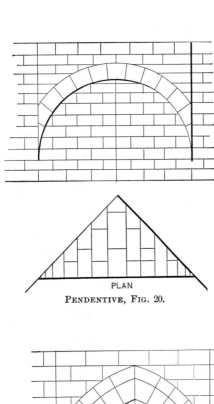

PLAN

PENDENTIVE, FIG. 20.

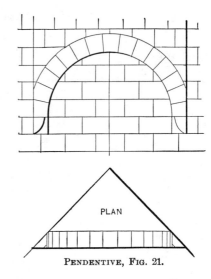

PLAN

PENDENTIVE, FIG. 21.

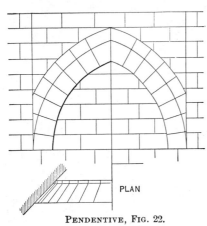

PLAN

PENDENTIVE, FIG. 22.

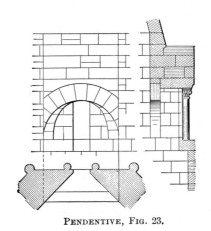

PENDENTIVE, FIG. 23.

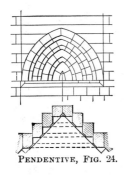

PENDENTIVE, FIG. 24.

PENDENTIVE, FIG. 25.

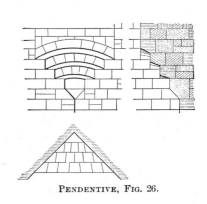

PENDENTIVE, FIG. 26.

260

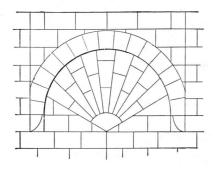

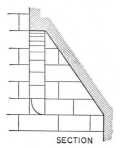

PENDENTIVE, Fig. 27.

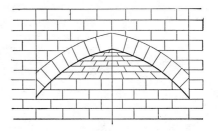

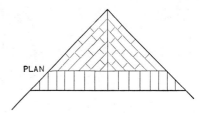

PLAN

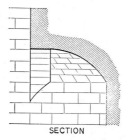

PENDENTIVE, Fig. 28.

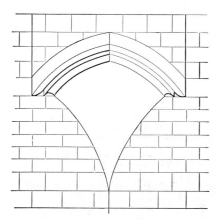

PENDENTIVE, Fig. 29.

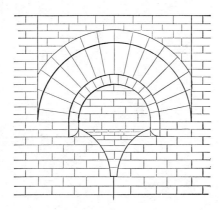

PENDENTIVE, Fig. 30.

PENDENTIVE BRACKETING: CON-
JECTURAL RESTORATION OF
ROOF OF AN ASSYRIAN CUPO-
LA, THE FORMS SUGGESTED
BY MOSLEM WORK.

261

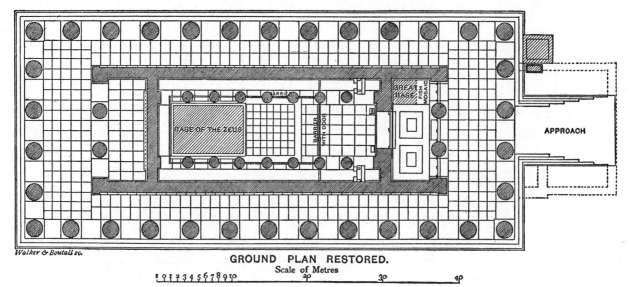

Walker & Boutall sc.

GROUND PLAN RESTORED.
Scale of Metres

PERIPTERAL TEMPLE: THAT OF ZEUS AT OLYMPIA.

The peristyle of 34 columns is separated from the naos by the width of the pteroma, and by the wider porticoes at the ends.

PERPENDICULAR ARCHITECTURE: EARLIEST TRACERY; EDINGTON, WILTSHIRE, A.D. 1361.

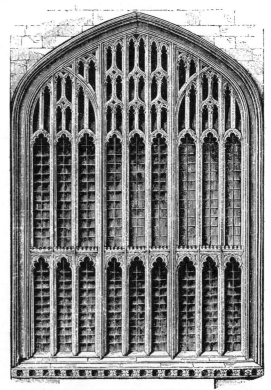

PERPENDICULAR ARCHITECTURE: LATE TRACERY; KING'S COLLEGE CHAPEL, CAMBRIDGE.

PERSIAN ARCHITECTURE, PART I.: PLATFORM AND RUINS AT PERSEPOLIS.

View from the east, that is, from a point below and to the left of *A* in the plan.   On the left are the winged human-headed bulls of the propylaea *B* in plan.   The columns are of the so-called hypostyle hall of Xerxes *E* on the second platform.

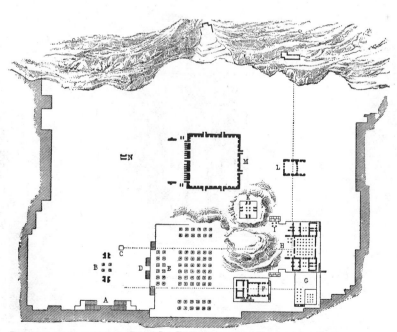

PERSIAN ARCHITECTURE, PART I.: PLATFORMS AND PALACES AT PERSEPOLIS.

The white surface is that of the platforms.

A Landing of stairs from town to platform.
B Propylaea on the first plateau.
C Cistern.
D Stairs leading to second plateau.
E So-called hypostyle hall of Xerxes.

F, G, H supposed royal dwellings (*F* generally called House of Darius).
I Gateway.
K Gateway.
L Unknown ruin.
M Throne room, called hall of 100 columns.

PEW: BINHAM PRIORY, NORFOLKSHIRE; C. 1340.

PEW IN CHURCH AT ELKSTONE,
GLOUCESTERSHIRE; C. 1280.

PEW IN CHURCH AT KIDLINGTON,
OXFORDSHIRE; WITH ABBREVIA-
TION OF THE NAME OF JESUS
(I.H.C.: SEE ARTICLE I.H.S.).

PEW: CHURCH AT STEEPLE AS-
TON, OXFORDSHIRE; C. 1500.

PEW: CHURCH AT MILVERTON, SOMER-
SETSHIRE, A.D. 1540.

The upper panel has the royal escutcheon, with the
Garter, Tudor Rose, and a Pomegranate.

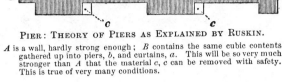
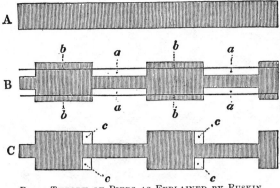
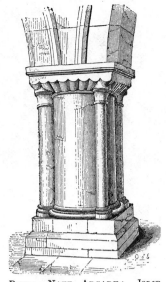

PIER: THEORY OF PIERS AS EXPLAINED BY RUSKIN.

A is a wall, hardly strong enough; *B* contains the same cubic contents gathered up into piers, *b*, and curtains, *a*. This will be so very much stronger than *A* that the material *c, c* can be removed with safety. This is true of very many conditions.

PIER: NAVE ARCADE; ISLIP CHURCH, OXFORDSHIRE; C. 1180.

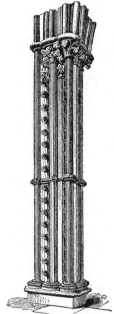

CLUSTERED AND BAND-ED PIER: CHOIR, LINCOLN CATHE-DRAL; C. 1200.

CLUSTERED PIER: ONLY THE VAULTING SHAFTS BANDED.

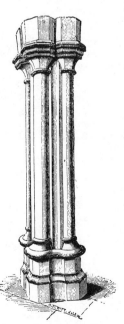

PIER: CLUSTERED PIER; OLD, NORTHAMPTON-SHIRE; C. 1450.

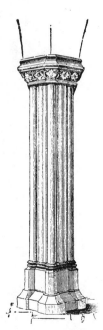

PIER: CLUSTERED PIER OF LATEST TYPE, WITH ONE CAPITAL FOR THE WHOLE. STOGUM-BER, CHURCH OF S. MARY, SOMER-SET; C. 1500.

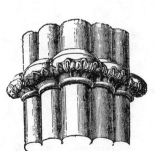

PIER: CLUSTERED AND BAND-ED PIERS; LINCOLN CATHE-DRAL; 13TH CENTURY.

265

PIERCED WORK: STONE WINDOW SLABS; CENTRAL SYRIA.

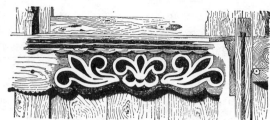

PIERCED WORK: SWITZERLAND, 17TH CENTURY.
Fascia below string course in wooden house; each piercing bordered by light coloured paintings.

PIGEON HOUSE: SHIRLY, VIRGINIA, U.S.
(Compare cuts under Colombier.)

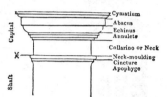

PILASTER: ROMAN DORIC, WITH NAMES OF THE DETAILS.

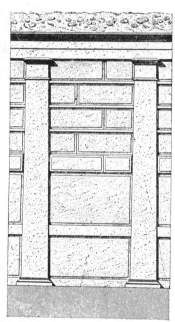

PILASTER OF DECORATIVE INTERIOR: PERISTYLE, HOUSE OF THE FAUN, POMPEII.

PILASTER: EARLY ROMANESQUE FORMS, 5TH CENTURY: EL BARAH, SYRIA.

  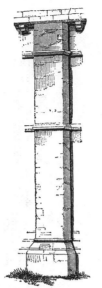 

PILASTER: LATE NEO-
CLASSIC, WROUGHT INTO
FORM OF GAINE; SCHLOSS
TORPA (WESTERGOTT-
LAND), SWEDEN.

PILASTER IN DECORA-
TIVE WOODWORK:
17TH CENTURY; WAD-
STENA, SWEDEN.

PILASTER STRIP: FOUN-
TAINS ABBEY; C.
1170.

PILLAR: NAVE ARCADE PIERS IN THE
FORM OF SIMPLE PILLARS; FOUN-
TAINS ABBEY, YORKSHIRE, ENGLAND;
C. 1180.

PILLAR: SQUARE AND ROUND ONES (COMMONLY CALLED PIERS
AND COLUMNS), KOKANAYA, SYRIA; 5TH CENTURY A.D.

PILLAR, OCTAGONAL:
CHURCH OF ORTON-ON-
THE-HILL, LEICESTER-
SHIRE; C. 1350.

PIN IN VISIBLE AND DEC-
ORATIVE FRAMING: A
SWISS CHALET.

The diagonal brace is halved
and notched into the upright,
and is held with two pins
with ornamental heads.

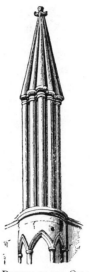

PINNACLE: OX-
FORD CATHE-
DRAL; c. 1220.

PINNACLE: PE-
TERBORO' CA-
THEDRAL, A.D.
1238.

PINNACLE: TOWER OF COUTANCES
CATHEDRAL, NORMANDY, ABOUT
1130, WITH PINNACLE OF UNUSUAL
SIZE.

The roof of the stair turret has also two pinnacles closely combined with its mass.

PINNACLE: WEST END OF ST. FRANCIS, PAVIA, 13TH CEN-
TURY, WITH PINNACLES OF WHOLLY DECORATIVE PUR-
POSE, AND UNUSUALLY HIGH.

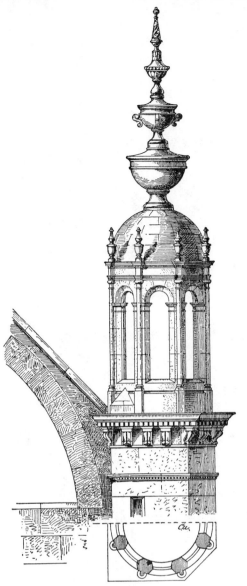

PINNACLE: SPANISH RENAISSANCE; CATHEDRAL
OF LEON; 1520–1550.

PISCINA: IN DWELLING-HOUSE AT OAKHAM, RUT-
LANDSHIRE; 13TH CENTURY.

PISCINA: COWLING CHURCH; C. 1260.

PISCINA: BLYTHFORD CHURCH, SUFFOLK; C. 1300.

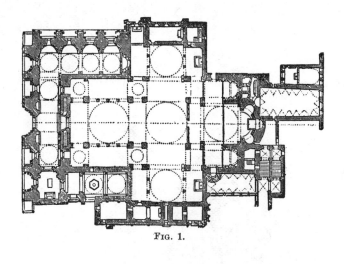

FIG. 1.

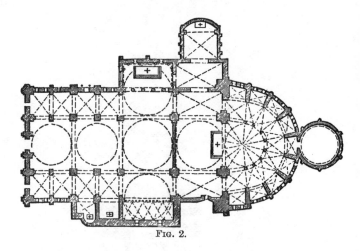

FIG. 2.

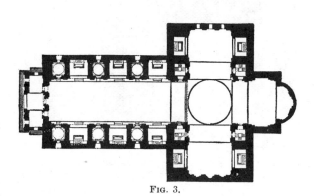

FIG. 3.

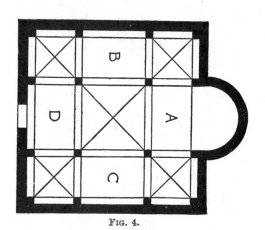

FIG. 4.

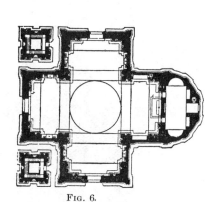

FIG. 6.

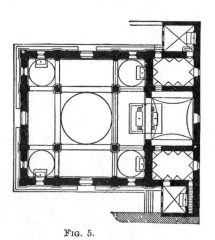

FIG. 5.

PLAN: A COMPARISON OF THE SYSTEMS OF THE FORMS OF CHURCH PLANS OF DIFFERENT EPOCHS. FOR THOSE OF THE BASILICA TYPE, OF ROMANESQUE, GOTHIC, RENAISSANCE, AND CINQUECENTO, SEE UNDER CHURCH AND SUBTITLES.

Fig. 1: Church of S. Mark, Venice, the typical Byzantine Greek cross with five cupolas with a narthex carried around the three sides of the western arm ; the southern branch of this cut off as a chapel. Fig. 2: S. Antonio, Padua, first half of thirteenth century ; a combined Romanesque and Byzantine style, though contemporaneous with the earlier Gothic buildings of North Italy ; the Greek cross is lost in the prolongations to east and west. Fig. 3: S. Andrea, Mantua ; c. 1475. One of the earliest Renaissance churches of wholly novel plan. The piers between the chapels serve as buttresses. Fig. 4: General scheme of Renaissance church plan in Middle Italy. A, B, C, D, are roofed by barrel vaults, the apse by a semidome, the five compartments either by groined vaults or cupolas. Compare Church of S. Fantino (plan under Church; interior under Renaissance). Fig. 5: Church of S. Maria Nuova, Cortona, Tuscany, the plan resembling Fig. 4 but with the chancel square-ended, covered by a cupola with lunettes flanked by sacristies. Fig. 6: S. Biagio, Montepulciano, Tuscany. The type plan Fig. 4 with the corner compartments omitted ; therefore reduced to the simplest terms, a Greek cross enclosed by walls as simple as a box, a single cupola, and four barrel vaults.

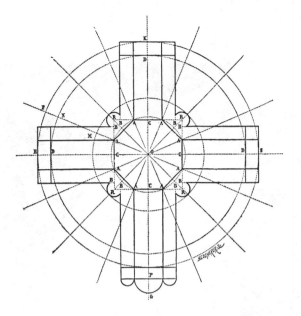

PLANNING: CHURCH AT KALAT SEM'AN, SYRIA;
5TH CENTURY.

O, column of S. Simeon Stylites. The circle *A, A, A*, fixes the Hypæthral octagon. The circle *R, R*, fixes the exterior of the absidioles. The circle *D, D*, fixes the length of the three great porches north, south, and west. The circle *H, K, S,* fixes the width of the outer narthex to each porch and the length of the nave of the church proper at the east. Lines drawn through *C, C*, are the axes of the church and porticoes. The sides of the naves and aisles being made parallel to these axes. Lines drawn through *R, R*, are the axes of the absidioles.

POLAND: ARCHITECTURE OF
KRAKAU (CRACOW), CHURCH
OF S. MARY.

POINTED ARCHITECTURE: HALL, MAYFIELD, ESSEX.

A building of the best Gothic period, but not intended for vaulting, and therefore not of Gothic Architecture in the strict sense.

gold mosaic

POLYCHROMY: MARBLES OF VARIED COLOUR; SPAN-
DRIL OF DOGE'S PALACE, VENICE.

POLYCHROMY: INLAY OF MARBLES AND COLOURED
AND GILDED GLASS; BASILICA OF S. CLEMENTE,
ROME.

POLYCHROMY: INLAY OF WOOD OF DIFFERENT
COLOURS (TARSIA).

POLYCHROMY: PAINTINGS OF HISTORICAL SUBJECT UNDER THE ROOF AND OF HERALDIC
SUBJECT ON EACH SIDE OF THE TRIPLE WINDOW COMBINED WITH COLOURED
TREATMENT OF THE HERALDIC AND OTHER CARVING AND A SOLIDLY GILDED
ROOF; INNSBRUCK, TYROL.

POLYCHROMY: PAINTING ON A FLAT CEILING OF
STOUT PLANK; SWEDISH; 17TH CENTURY.

POLYCHROMY: PAINTING ON A PLASTER CEILING;
17TH CENTURY NORTHERN WORK.

But the pattern is derived from the endless supply of diapers
and sowings in Italian and Spanish tiles and stencil work.

POPPY-HEAD: CLIFTON CAMPVILLE CHURCH, STAF-
FORDSHIRE; RUDE 14TH CENTURY WORK.

POLYGON OF FORCES.

POPPY-HEAD: ALL SOUL'S
CHAPEL, OXFORD; C.
1450.

POPPY-HEAD: CHRIST CHURCH, OXFORD;
c. 1520.

274

PORCH: CHURCH AT BARNACK, NORTHAMP-
TONSHIRE; C. 1250.

PORCH: CHURCH AT BERNIÈRES (CALVADOS); C. 1250.

PORCH: TIMBER CONSTRUCTION, ALDHAM, ESSEX; C. 1350.

PORCH: KIDLINGTON CHURCH, OXFORDSHIRE; C. 1350.
The inner doorway is much earlier.

PORCH: WOODEN CANOPY WITHOUT PILLARS; 15TH CENTURY.
HOSPITAL AT BEAUNE IN BURGUNDY.

PORCH: ALL SAINTS, STAMFORD, LINCOLNSHIRE;
C. 1500.

PORCH: AMERICAN "OLD COLONIAL" OR GEOR-
GIAN ARCHITECTURE; LITCHFIELD, CONN.

PORTE COCHÈRE AT TOULOUSE: C. 1580.

PORTE COCHÈRE: RUE BOURDONNAIS, PARIS; 16TH CENTURY
STYLE OF LOUIS XIV.

PORTE COCHÈRE SEEN FROM WITHIN; ENTRANCES TO THE HOUSES AT LEFT AND RIGHT; MODERN PARIS.

POT CHIMNEY: AS BUILT BY INDIANS IN THE N.W. OF THE U.S.

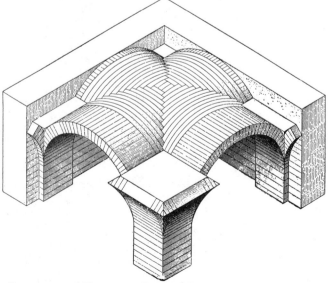

PROJECTION: A BYZANTINE GROINED VAULT SHOWN IN ISOMETRIC PROJECTION.

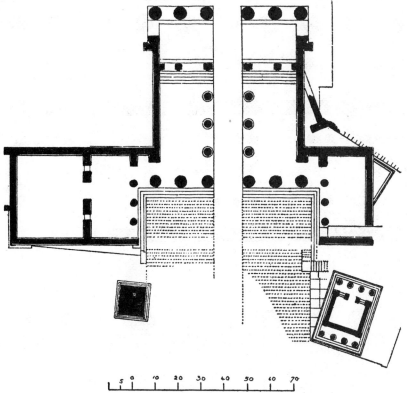

PROPYLAIA OF ACROPOLIS AT ATHENS.

The dotted lines show steps which were probably absent in classical times. The path through the middle seems to have been kept open for beasts of burden. The three columns on each side of this path are Ionic: all the rest of the building is Doric. The little building on the right is the Ionic temple of the Wingless Victory.

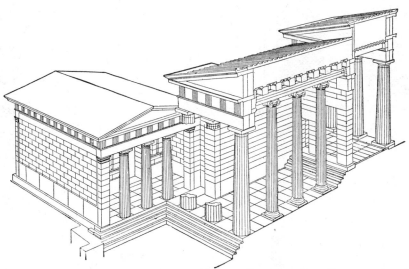

PROPYLAIA AT ATHENS: PERSPECTIVE SECTION SHOWING NORTHERN HALF RESTORED (SEE PLAN).

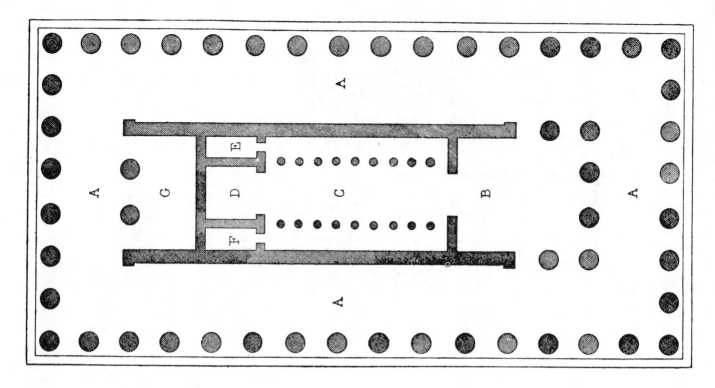

PSEUDO-DIPTERAL TEMPLE AT SELINUS, SICILY: 5TH CENTURY B.C.

PULPIT: S. MINIATO, NEAR FLORENCE; INLAY OF
BLACK AND WHITE MARBLE; DESIGN PROB-
ABLY OF 12TH CENTURY.

PULPIT: ENTRANCE FROM STAIRWAY IN THE
WALL, BEAULIEU, HANTS; c. 1260.

PULPIT: CHURCH OF S. GIOVANNI AT PISTOIA; C. 1270.
The sculptures by Niccolò Pisano or his pupils.

PULPIT OF OAK: FOTHERINGAY CHURCH, NORTH-
AMPTONSHIRE; A.D. 1440.

PULPIT: EXTERNAL, ADJOINING DOORWAY OF
BAPTISTERY, PISTOIA; C. 1350.

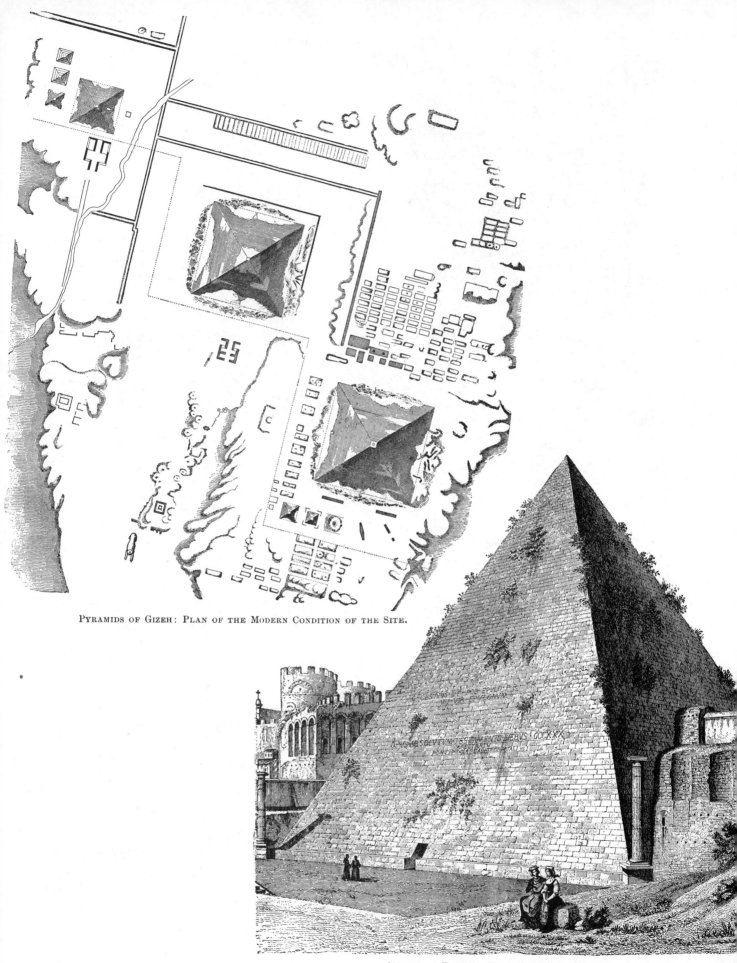

PYRAMIDS OF GIZEH: PLAN OF THE MODERN CONDITION OF THE SITE.

PYRAMID: TOMB OF CAIUS CESTIUS AT ROME.

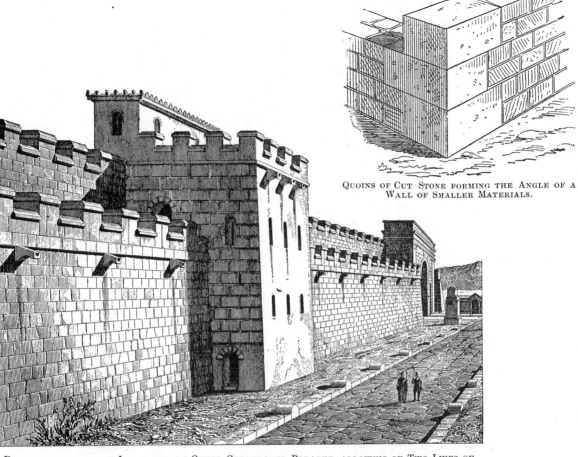

QUOINS OF CUT STONE FORMING THE ANGLE OF A
WALL OF SMALLER MATERIALS.

RAMPART CARRYING AN INNER AND AN OUTER CRENELATED PARAPET, ALLOWING OF TWO LINES OF
BOWMEN, ETC. WALLS OF POMPEII, CAMPANIA, ITALY; PROBABLY C. 200 B.C.

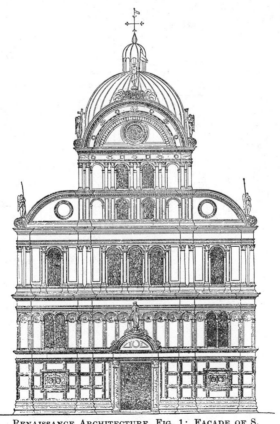

RENAISSANCE ARCHITECTURE, FIG. 1: FAÇADE OF S.
ZACCARIA, VENICE; C. 1490.

RENAISSANCE ARCHITECTURE, FIG. 2: THE MANOR HOUSE OF THE MERCHANT ANGO, NEAR VARENGE-
VILLE, SEINE INFÉRIEURE, FRANCE; c. 1530.
Early French Renaissance manifested in simple country buildings.

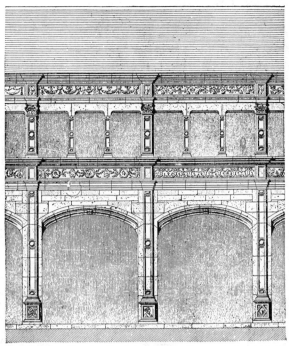

RENAISSANCE ARCHITECTURE, FIG. 3: CHÂTEAU BUSSY-RABUTIN, ARCADE ON COURT; C. 1540.

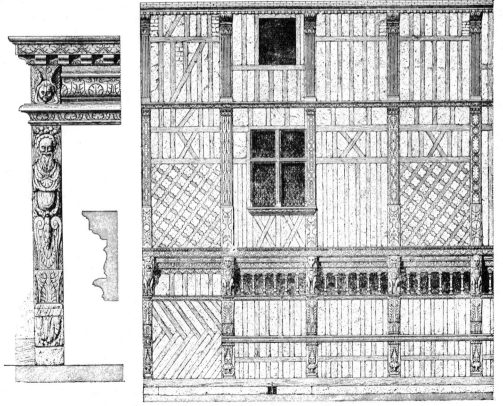

RENAISSANCE ARCHITECTURE, FIG. 4: HOUSE AT BEAUVAIS; C. 1560.
French Renaissance seen in wood-framed street architecture.

RENAISSANCE ARCHITECTURE, FIG. 5: HOUSE AT
ROUEN; C. 1581.

This and Fig. 6 are of the latest epoch of Renaissance; the
style Henri Quatre succeeds it immediately.

RENAISSANCE ARCHITECTURE, FIG. 6: HOUSE AT AMIENS, 1593; SEE FIG. 5.

REREDOS, FIG. 1: SOMERTON, OXFORDSHIRE; C. 1400.
In this case, as in Fig. 2, the altar has been moved, but the reredos keeps its ancient place.

REREDOS, FIG. 2: S. THOMAS'S CHURCH, SALISBURY; C. 1450.

RIB, FIG. 1: EARLY RIBBED VAULTING WITH ONLY THE ESSENTIAL RIBS, VIZ., DIAGONAL RIBS (OGIVES) MEETING AT THE CENTRAL BOSS; TRANSVERSE RIBS SEPARATING THE VAULTING SQUARES; WALL RIBS (FORMERETS) ON RIGHT AND LEFT; THE COMPARTMENT IN THE DISTANCE IS, IN PART, IN SEXPARTITE VAULTING; SALISBURY CATHEDRAL.

RIB, FIG. 2: VAULTING OF 1260 WITH MANY RIBS USED FOR ORNAMENT ALONE, AS THOSE AT THE RIDGE OF THE VAULT. AND ALL THE OTHERS NOT FOUND IN FIG. 1: WESTMINSTER ABBEY.

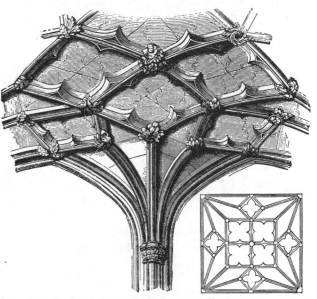

RIB, FIG. 3: ROOF WITH RIBS LARGELY NON-CONSTRUCTIONAL; ENGLISH PERPENDICULAR STYLE; LIERNE VAULT, S. MARY REDCLIFFE, BRISTOL; A.D., 1413.

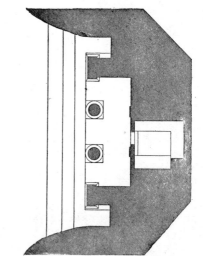

ROCK-CUT BUILDING: TOMB AT TELMISSUS, ASIA
MINOR; PLAN.

ROCK-CUT BUILDING: TOMB AT TELMISSUS; SEE
PLAN.

ROCK-CUT BUILDING: UNDERGROUND KITCHEN, VILLAGE OF MONDJEBIA, SYRIA.

ROCOCO ARCHITECTURE: EARLIEST TYPE; DOORWAY AT
TOULOUSE, FRANCE.

ROCOCO ARCHITECTURE: EARLY AND GOOD DECORATION FROM A CHÂTEAU AT BERCY, PARIS; NOW
DESTROYED.

ROCOCO ARCHITECTURE: PERFECTED INTERIOR DECORATION; c. 1760; BRUCHSAL ON THE RHINE.

ROCOCO ARCHITECTURE: STOCKHOLM, SWEDEN.

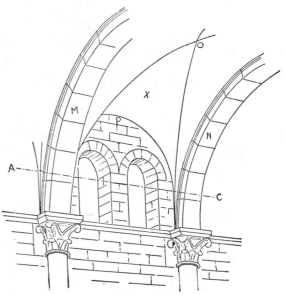

ROMANESQUE ARCHITECTURE: VAULTING COMMON IN GER-
MAN ROMANESQUE CHURCHES.

M N, transverse arches; *A C*, springing line of the smaller arch of the
vault; *P*, crown of the smaller arch; *X*, triangle of vaulting which is
curved in the direction *O* to *P* as well as in the opposite way.

ROMANESQUE ARCHITECTURE: CHURCH OF VIGNORY; SEE PLAN.

ROMANESQUE ARCHITECTURE: ENGLISH, C. 1140; CHURCH AT NORTHAMPTON.

ROMANESQUE ARCHITECTURE: A DOMED CHURCH; S. FRONT AT PÉRIGUEUX (DORDOGNE); 13TH CENTURY.

ROMANESQUE ARCHITECTURE: PISCINA, KIRK-
STALL ABBEY, YORKSHIRE; c. 1160.

ROMANESQUE ARCHITECTURE: PORCH, KELSO
ABBEY, SCOTLAND; c. 1160.

ROMANESQUE ARCHITECTURE: CAPITALS OF PORCH, ST. PETER'S
CHURCH, NORTHAMPTON; c. 1160.

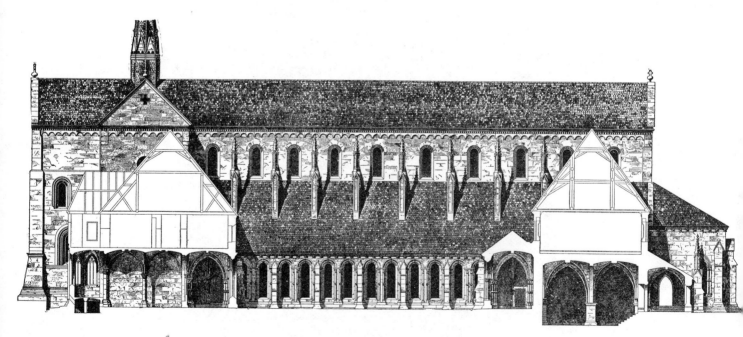

ROMANESQUE ARCHITECTURE: ABBEY CHURCH AT
MAULBRON.
See the ground plan under Monastic Architecture.

292

ROMANESQUE ARCHITECTURE: CAPITAL IN CHURCH OF MAURSMÜNS-
TER NEAR STRALSBURG.

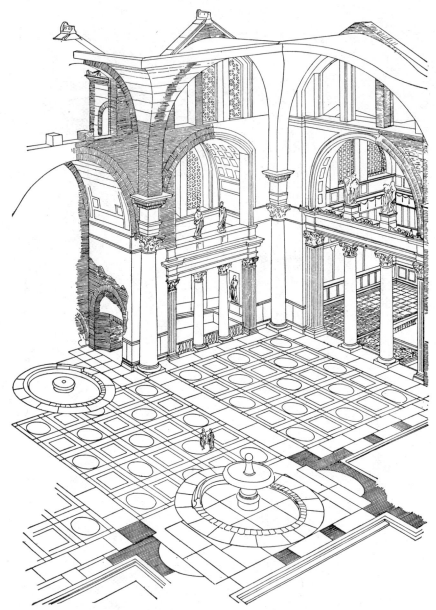

ROMAN IMPERIAL ARCHITECTURE: THERMÆ OF CARACALLA; C. 215 A.D.
Viollet-le-Duc's restoration of the great hall (tepidarium).

294

ROMAN IMPERIAL ARCHITECTURE: A HALL OF THE THERMÆ OF DIOCLETIAN; C. 300 A.D.

The groined vault has lost its ornaments, but the walls and piers are nearly as originally designed.   (This is now the church of S. Maria degli Angeli.)

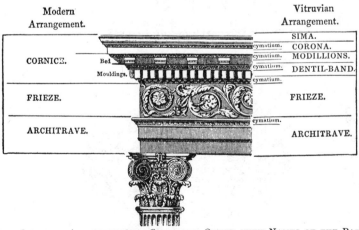

ROMAN IMPERIAL ARCHITECTURE: COMPOSITE ORDER WITH NAMES OF THE PARTS.

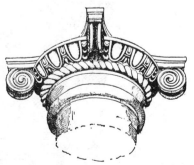

ROMAN IMPERIAL ARCHITECTURE: IONIC CAPITAL, TEMPLE OF SATURN IN THE ROMAN FORUM.

ROMAN IMPERIAL ARCHITECTURE: COLUMNS FROM
THE TEMPLE OF DIANA, EVORA, PORTUGAL.

An illustration of principal and declining style.

ROMAN IMPERIAL ARCHITECTURE: CORINTHIAN CAPITAL
WITH IMAGERY; PRESERVED IN THE LATERAN MUSEUM,
ROME.

ROMAN IMPERIAL ARCHITECTURE: CAPITALS OF LATE EPOCH USED BY THE MOORISH BUILDERS OF
THE MOSQUE AT CORDOVA.

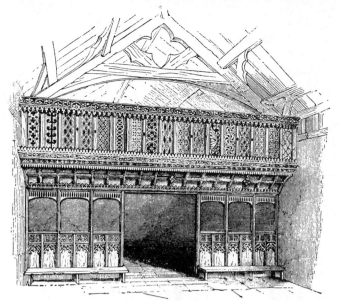

ROOD LOFT: LLANEGRYNN, MERIONETHSHIRE; C. 1500.
The cross (rood) is no longer in place; perhaps removed during the Puritan supremacy.

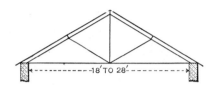
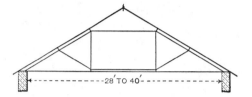

18' TO 28'

28' TO 40'

ROOF: FLAT, AS USED IN NEARLY RAINLESS REGIONS; DOUMA, SYRIA. SEE FIRST CUT UNDER SYRIA.

ROOF OF STONE; SLABS RESTING ON CROSS WALLS
CARRIED ON ARCHES.
For similar transverse arches see cuts Monastic Architecture;
Pointed Architecture.

297

ROOF: WITH COLLAR BEAMS AND BRACES (KNEE RAFTERS), 13TH CENTURY; HALL OF STOKESAY
CASTLE, SHROPSHIRE.

ROOF: EARLY ENGLISH; SOLAR OF HOUSE AT CHARNEY, BERKSHIRE; c. 1270; WITH CAMBERED
CROSS BEAMS SUPPORTING POSTS AND A PURLIN PLATE BY DIRECT RESISTANCE TO PRESSURE;
13TH CENTURY.

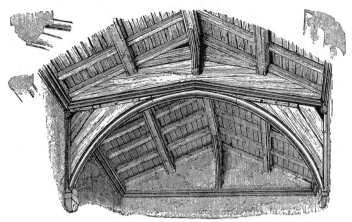

ROOF: FRAMED LIKE A FLOOR: HEAVY CROSS BEAMS CARRYING PURLINS, AND STIFFENED BY BRACES CUT TO A CURVE WHICH IS COMPLETED BY MOULDINGS PLANTED ON; KIDDINGTON, OXON; c. 1350.

ROOF: WITH CAMBERED CROSS BEAMS CARRYING A DECORATIVE SYSTEM OF BRACES AND STRUTS.

ROOF: LIKE THAT AT CHARNEY, BUT MUCH LIGHTER AS BEING WORK OF A SKILLED CONSTRUCTOR; HIGHAM FERRERS, NORTHAMPTONSHIRE; c. 1350.

ROOF: OF STAIRCASE, THORNTON ABBEY, LINCOLNSHIRE; C. 1370.

ROOF: ELABORATE HAMMER-BEAM CONSTRUCTION; S. STEPHEN'S
CHURCH, NORWICH; C. 1480.

ROSACE FROM A HOUSE AT BETOURSA, SYRIA;
5TH TO 6TH CENTURY.

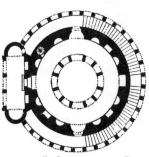

ROUND CHURCH: S. COSTANZA AT ROME; PLAN.

ROUND CHURCH: S. COSTANZA AT ROME; SEE PLAN.

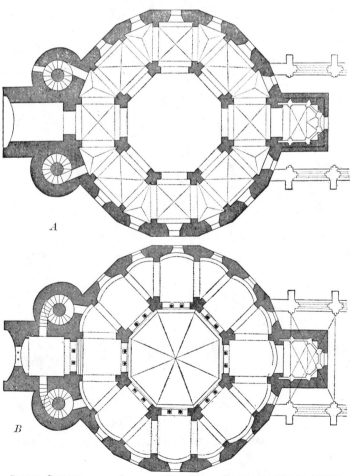

ROUND CHURCH: THE ORIGINAL CHAPEL OF CHARLEMAGNE AT AIX-LA-
CHAPELLE; *A*, GROUND STORY; *B*, UPPER STORY.

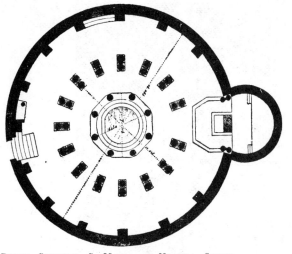

ROUND CHURCH: S. MARIA AT NOCERA, SOUTH
ITALY; 6TH CENTURY A.D.; PLAN.

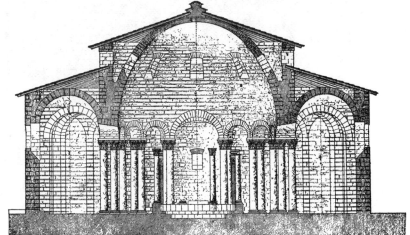

ROUND CHURCH: S. MARIA AT NOCERA; SEE PLAN.

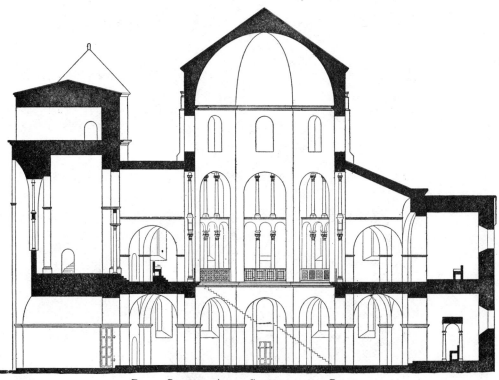

ROUND CHURCH: AIX-LA-CHAPELLE; SEE PLANS.

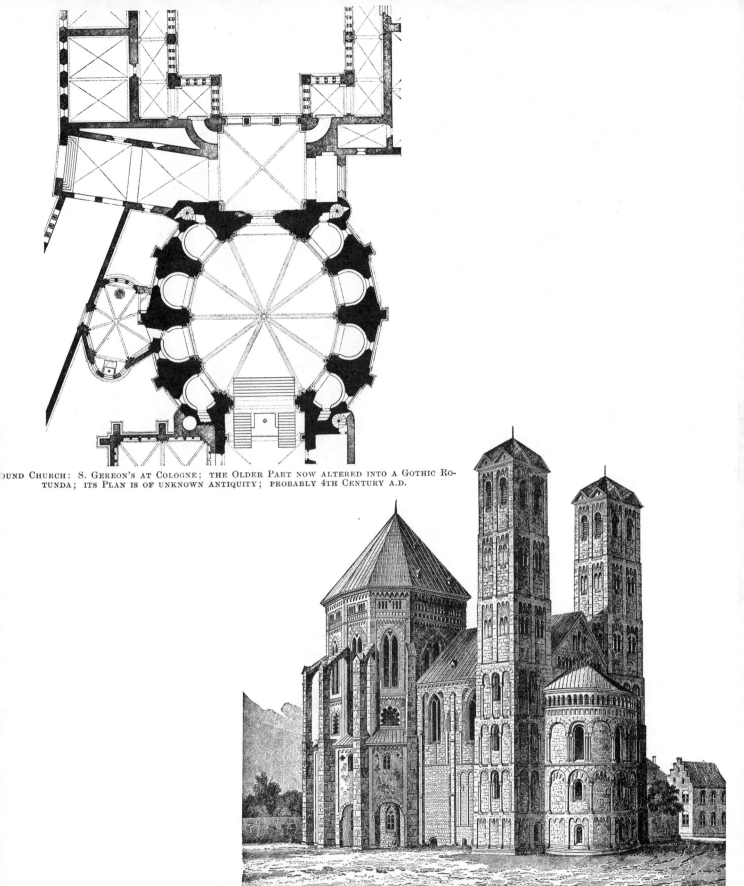

ROUND CHURCH: S. GEREON'S AT COLOGNE; THE OLDER PART NOW ALTERED INTO A GOTHIC RO-
TUNDA; ITS PLAN IS OF UNKNOWN ANTIQUITY; PROBABLY 4TH CENTURY A.D.

ROUND CHURCH: S. GEREON'S AT COLOGNE, FROM THE S.E.; SEE PLAN.
The smaller accessory buildings are not shown.

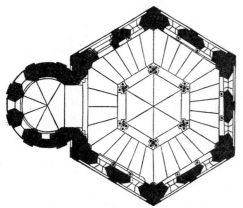

ROUND CHURCH: MATHIAS KAPELLE AT KOBERN
ON THE RHINE; PLAN.

ROUND CHURCH: MATHIAS KAPELLE: SECTION
SHOWING INTERIOR ONLY; SEE PLAN.

ROUND TOWER (DEF. *A*): ARDMORE, IRELAND.

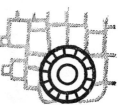

ROUND TOWER (DEF. *B*).

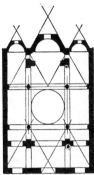

RUSSIA, FIG. 1: A GREEK BYZANTINE CHURCH-PLAN, ILLUSTRATING THE TYPE COMMON IN RUSSIA ALSO; THE CUPOLA IS COMMONLY LIKE THAT SHOWN IN FIG. 2.

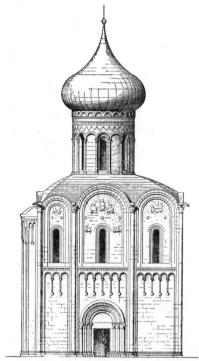

RUSSIA, FIG. 2: CHURCH OF THE INTERCESSION OF THE VIRGIN AT POKROVA; SEE THE GREEK PLAN, FIG. 1.

RUSSIA, FIG. 3: TOWER OF CHURCH OF VASILI BLAJENOI, MOSCOW; RECEDING ARCHES DIMINISHING SIZE OF CENTRAL OPENING.

RUSSIA, FIG. 4: TOWER OF S. JOHN CHRYSOSTOM, AT JAROSLAW; SHOWING INDIAN INFLUENCE.

RUSSIA, FIG. 5: LOG BUILT HOUSE, PROVINCE OF KOSTRUMA.

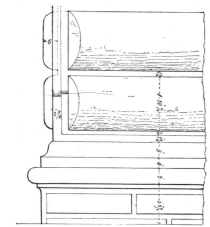

RUSTICATION: BASE OF PALAZZO STROZZI, FLORENCE; 15TH CENTURY.

RUSTICATION: PALAZZO WIDMAN, VENICE, ITALY; CLOSE OF 16TH CENTURY.

SACRISTY: CATHEDRAL OF LE MANS (SARTHE), FRANCE.

SAINTE CHAPELLE: S. GERMER NEAR BEAUVAIS (OISE), FRANCE; AT EAST END OF CHURCH

SARCOPHAGUS OF ROMAN IMPERIAL TIME FROM TOMB OF CECILIA METELLA NEAR ROME: NOW PRESERVED IN THE PALAZZO FARNESE.

SCABELLUM WITH DECORATIVE VASE; MODERN
FRENCH.

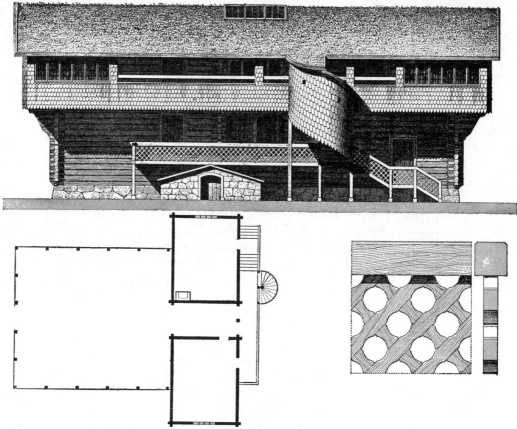

SCANDINAVIA, FIG. 1 : HOUSE IN WHICH GUSTAVUS WASA TOOK REFUGE IN 1529; NEAR UPSALA, SWEDEN.

The structure is of solid timber like a log house, or a châlet of type *a*.   Part of upper story and screen of stairs are covered
with large, matched shingles.

SCANDINAVIA, FIG. 2: HOUSE OF GUSTAVUS WASA; SEE FIG. 1.

SCANDINAVIA, FIG. 3: SWEDISH HOUSE, CLOSE OF
17TH CENTURY.

The roofing has been carried over the coping of the gable, in-
juring the outline : compare Fig. 4.

SCANDINAVIA, FIG. 4: 17TH CENTURY DOORWAY,
CASTLE TORPA, WESTGÖTLAND, SWEDEN.

The heraldic achievements are unusually well disposed.

SCANDINAVIA, FIG. 5; SWEDISH DECORATION OF
INLAID WOOD; PALACE AT KALMAR.

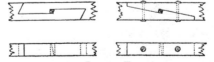

SCARF, AS USED IN JOINING TIMBERS, WHICH ARE
THEN SAID TO BE SCARFED.

SCOTLAND: ABBEY OF IONA, SOUTH AISLE OF CHOIR; DIVIDED INTO THREE COMPARTMENTS BY TWO
FLYING BUTTRESSES OF PRIMITIVE TYPE.

SCOTLAND: JEDBURGH ABBEY; PART OF CHOIR.

SCOTLAND: KELSO ABBEY; NAVE AND SOUTH TRANSEPT FROM N.E.

SCREEN, FIG. 1: LOW BRONZE RAILING, AIX-LA-CHAPELLE; PROBABLY 5TH CENTURY, AND FROM ITALY.

SCREEN, FIG. 2: SEE FIG. 1.

SCREEN, FIG. 4: SEE FIG. 3 OF WHICH THIS IS A
PARTIAL ENLARGEMENT.

SCREEN OF OAK: NORTHFLEET CHURCH, KENT; C. 1300.

SCREEN, FIG. 3: SEE FIGS. 1 AND 2, THIS BEING A DETAIL OF A THIRD AND VERY SIMILAR SCREEN.

A   *B*

SCREENS OF OAK: *A*, SHOTSWELL, OXFORDSHIRE; C. 1350. *B*, GEDDINGTON, NORTHAMPTONSHIRE; C. 1360.

Screen of Cut Stone dividing a Chapel: Cathedral of
Aix-la-Chapelle; 14th Century.

Screen of Oak: Handborough Church, Oxfordshire; c. 1480.

Screen serving as Choir Screen: Fyfield Church, Berkshire;
c. 1480.

SCULPTURE, FIG. 1: ASSYRIAN (SEE MESOPOTAMIA): ALABASTER SLAB FROM SENNACHERIB'S PALACE, MOUND OF KOUYUNJIK.

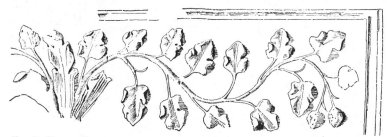

SCULPTURE, FIG. 2: ROMAN FRIEZE PROBABLY OF TIME OF AUGUSTUS; IN THE LATERAN MUSEUM, ROME.

SCULPTURE, FIG. 4: ITALIAN ROMANESQUE, 12TH CENTURY; CHURCH OF S. ANDREA, PISTOJA.

SCULPTURE, FIG. 13: FRENCH GOTHIC; BOURGES CATHEDRAL; WINDOW OVER WEST PORTAL.

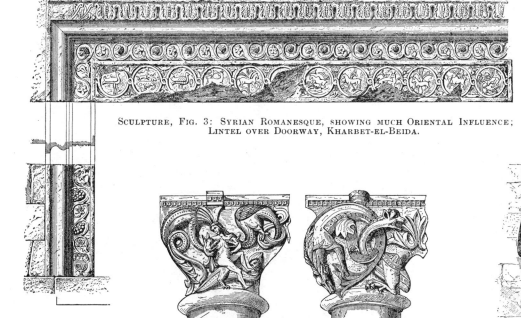

SCULPTURE, FIG. 3: SYRIAN ROMANESQUE, SHOWING MUCH ORIENTAL INFLUENCE;
LINTEL OVER DOORWAY, KHARBET-EL-BEIDA.

SCULPTURE, FIGS. 5 AND 6: GERMAN ROMANESQUE; CHURCH
AT BRAUWEILER ON THE RHINE.

SCULPTURE, FIG. 7: GERMAN ROMANESQUE; 12TH
CENTURY; PORTRAIT EFFIGY; ABBEY OF ARN-
STEIN ON THE RHINE.

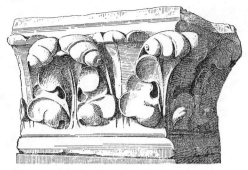

SCULPTURE, FIG. 8: FRENCH GOTHIC CORNICE; 13TH CENTURY.

SCULPTURE, FIG. 9: FRENCH GOTHIC CORNICE; 13TH CENTURY.

SCULPTURE, FIG. 10: FRENCH GOTHIC; BURGUNDIAN SCHOOL; CROCKETS OF A CAPITAL.

SCULPTURE, FIG. 11: FRENCH GOTHIC; BURGUNDIAN SCHOOL; ONE CROCKET OF A CAPITAL.

SCULPTURE, FIG. 12: FRENCH GOTHIC; CATHEDRAL OF CHARTRES; BASE IN NORTH PORCH.

SCULPTURE, FIG. 14: CANOPY OF THE BISHOP'S
THRONE; ANCIENT CARVED OAK STALLS;
CATHEDRAL OF PALERMO.

SCULPTURE, FIG. 15: LATE ITALIAN GOTHIC; CLOSE OF THE 14TH CENTURY;
VITERBO, ITALY.

SCULPTURE, FIG. 16: FRENCH RENAISSANCE;
EARLIEST PERIOD; TOMB OF PHILIPPE DE
COMINES; ABOUT 1510.

SCUTCHEON: PIERCED AND WROUGHT IRON; C.
1450; BEAUCHAMP CHAPEL, WARWICK.

SCUTCHEON OF SHEET IRON WITH WROUGHT IRON
DROP HANDLE; C. 1480; RYARSH CHURCH,
KENT.

SEDILIA WITH PISCINA; C. 1200; RUSHDEN CHURCH,
NORTHAMPTONSHIRE.

SEDILIA: C. 1250; UFFINGTON CHURCH, BERKSHIRE.

SHAFT OF DOUBLE
FUSIFORM SHAPE,
CARVED WITH LEAF-
AGE: CLOISTER AT
BELEM, PORTUGAL.

MIDWALL SHAFT: WINDOW IN CHURCH OF
GERNRODE, GERMANY.

MIDWALL SHAFT: ABBEY OF MÜNSTERMAIFELD, RHENISH
PRUSSIA.

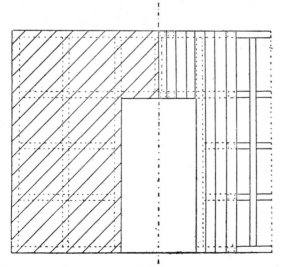

SHEATHING, DIAGONAL AND VERTICAL, AS WITH ROUGH
BOARDS ON A FRAME OF STUDS AND TIES; THE SCHEME
SHOWN IS GERMAN.

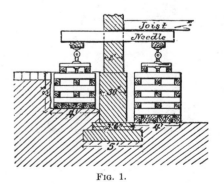

FIG. 1.

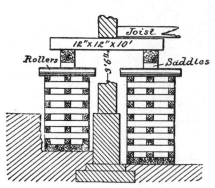

Joist.
12"x12"x10'
Rollers
Saddles

FIG. 2.

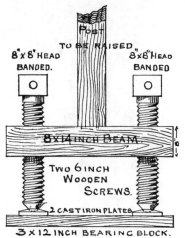

POST
TO BE RAISED
8"x8" HEAD
BANDED.
8"x8" HEAD
BANDED
8x14 INCH BEAM.
TWO 6 INCH
WOODEN
SCREWS.
2 CAST IRON PLATES
3 x 12 INCH BEARING BLOCK.

FIG. 3.

24x3x¾-inch Pitch.
FIG. 4.

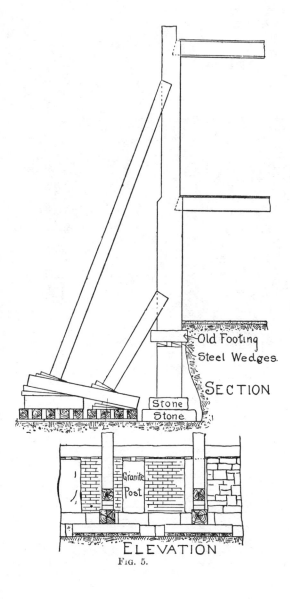

Old Footing
Steel Wedges.
SECTION
Stone
Stone
Granite
Post
ELEVATION
FIG. 5.

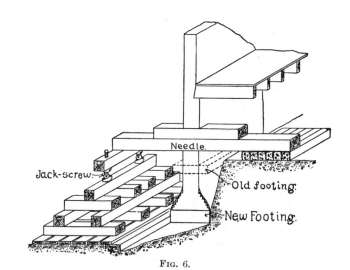

Needle.
Jack-screw.
Old footing.
New Footing.

FIG. 6.

FIG. 7.

SKEW VAULT OR ARCH: THE TRIANGLE IN THE PLAN CORRESPONDS TO THE ELABORATE HORIZONTAL MOULDINGS IN THE VIEW, WHICH ARE THE CORBELLING TO CARRY THE WALL ABOVE.

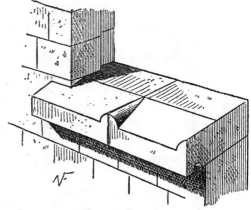

SILL FOR A WINDOW OPENING: OF STONE CUT WITH A WASH, WITH LUGS UNDER THE JAMB STONES AND SADDLE JOINTS.

SOMERSET HOUSE, LONDON: VESTIBULE; AFTER 1776 A.D.

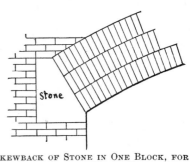

SKEWBACK OF STONE IN ONE BLOCK, FOR A BRICK ARCH IN THREE ROLLOCKS.

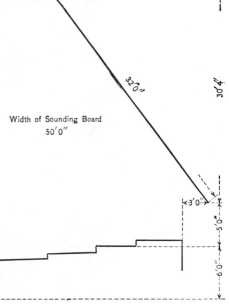

SOUNDING BOARD IN SENSE *B* (MORE PROPERLY REFLECTOR): AS DESCRIBED UNDER MUSIC HALL (5); THE DIMENSIONS ARE GIVEN IN FEET AND INCHES.

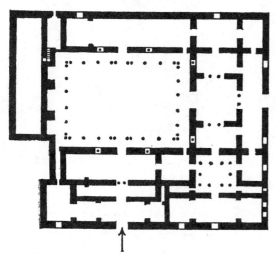

SPAIN, ARCHITECTURE OF: PLAN OF THE ALCAZAR, SEVILLE. MOORISH IN ORIGIN, ILLUSTRATING THE USE OF THE PATIO FROM WHICH LARGE ROOMS ARE ENTERED AND TAKE DAYLIGHT.

SPAIN, ARCHITECTURE OF; ARCADES ON PATIO; PALACE AT GUADALAJARA; ABOUT 1465 A.D.

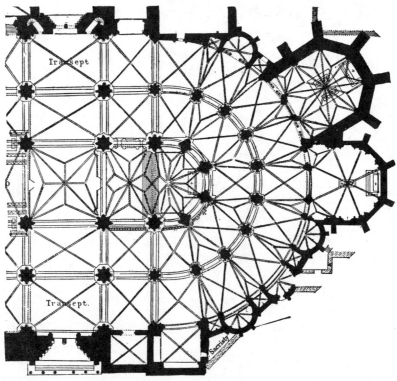

SPAIN, ARCHITECTURE OF: CHOIR AND AISLES OF TOLEDO CATHEDRAL; BEGINNING OF THE 14TH CENTURY. THE ALTERNATION OF SQUARES AND TRIANGLES IN THE VAULTING OF DEAMBULATORY IS VERY RARE; IT OCCURS ALSO IN THE CATHEDRAL OF LE MANS IN FRANCE.

SPAIN, ARCHITECTURE OF: PALACE OF CHARLES V., GRANADA; BEGUN ABOUT 1530 A.D.; NEVER
FINISHED.

SPAIN, ARCHITECTURE OF: CATHEDRAL OF JAEN, BEGUN 1532. THE WEST FRONT AND TOWERS,
THIRTY YEARS LATER; ONE OF THE FINEST NEOCLASSIC DESIGNS.

SPAIN, ARCHITECTURE OF: SANTIAGO DE COMPOSTELLA: CATHEDRAL, WEST FAÇADE, 1680.

SPAIN, ARCHITECTURE OF: COURT OF THE ROYAL PALACE
AT MADRID; ABOUT 1730 A.D.

SPEOS OF RAMSES II. AT ABU SIMBEL, UPPER EGYPT.

SPIRE OF CHURCH: BERNIÈRES
(CALVADOS); 13TH CENTURY.

SPIRE OF NORTH TOWER, CHARTRES CATHEDRAL:
FINISHED 1513: HEIGHT ABOUT 380 FEET.

SPIRE OF SOUTH TOWER, CHARTRES CATHEDRAL: c. 1175;
HEIGHT ABOUT 350 FEET.

325

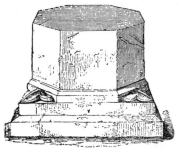 

SPUR: ENGLISH ROMANESQUE; ROCHESTER CATHEDRAL; c. 1120.

SPUR: ENGLISH GOTHIC, EARLIEST TYPE; S. CROSS, WINCHESTER.

SPUR: ENGLISH GOTHIC; 13TH CENTURY; STOCK-BURY, KENT.

SQUINCH: OXFORD CATHEDRAL; c. 1240.

SQUINCH: SALISBURY CATHEDRAL; c. 1300.

326

SQUINT: CRAWLEY CHURCH, HAMPSHIRE; 13TH
CENTURY; THE SILL SERVES AS A PISCINA.

SQUINT: S. MARY MAGDALEN, TAUNTON; 14TH
CENTURY.

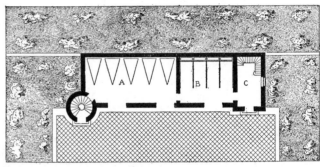

GROUND STORY: *A*, CARRIAGE HOUSE; *B*, STABLE; *C*, HARNESS
ROOM.

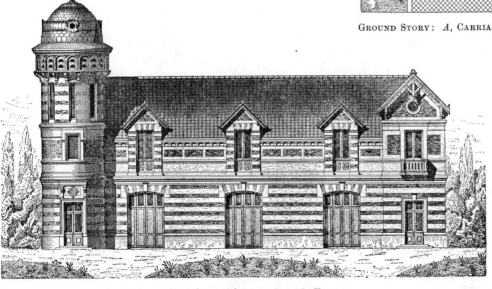

STABLE AT MÂCON (SÂONE-ET-LOIRE), FRANCE.

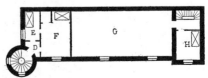

UPPER STORY: *D*, LANDING; *E*, *F*, *H*, BED
ROOMS; *G*, FODDER LOFT.

327

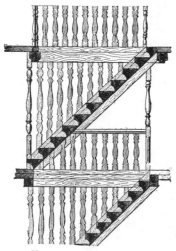

STAIRS IN A HOUSE AT WOLFENSCHIESSEN, SWITZ-
ERLAND. EACH STEP IS A SOLID TIMBER: ITS
ENDS FRAMED INTO THE STRING PIECES.

CATHEDRAL OF SENS (YONNE). STAIRCASE TO UPPER SACRISTY
TRANSITION; 12TH CENTURY.

STAIRCASE AT PÉRIGUEUX (DORDOGNE): NEOCLASSIC OF 17TH CENTURY, WITH LOCAL PECULIARITIES
OF DETAIL.

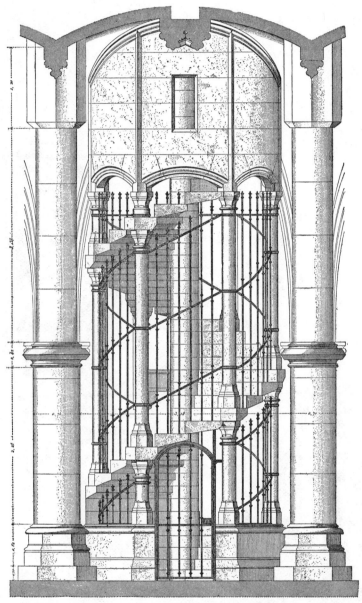

PALAIS DE JUSTICE, PARIS. THE CAGE IS CYLINDRICAL, AND PIERCES THE VAULTED FLOOR BELOW AND
ABOVE. THE IRONWORK IS INTENDED TO SEPARATE THE STAIRWAY COMPLETELY FROM THE CORRI-
DORS; THERE IS A GATE AT EVERY LANDING.

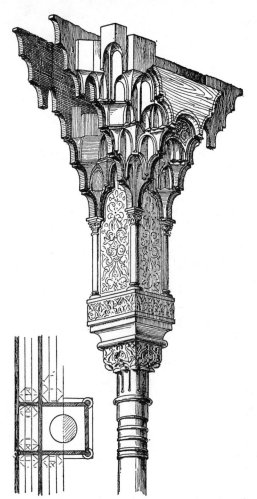

STALACTITE WORK IN WOOD AND PLASTER: THE
ALHAMBRA, GRANADA, SPAIN.

STALLS OF S. GEREON, COLOGNE: 14TH CENTURY; TYPICAL GOTHIC ARRANGE
AND DESIGN; THE HEAVY SEAT IN EACH STALL IS A MISERERE.

STAIR TURRET: CHURCH OF S. WULFRAN, ABBE-
VILLE (SOMME).

STALLS: S. MARGARET'S CHURCH, LEICESTERSHIRE;
c. 1450.

STALLS, CARVED OAK: MONTRÉAL (YONNE), BURGUNDY; EARLY RENAISSANCE; c. 1520.

STALLS IN THE CHURCH OF NOTRE DAME, PARIS;
17TH CENTURY.

STEEPLE OF A CHURCH NEAR CAEN IN NOR-
MANDY: c. 1160.

STILTED ARCH: CHURCH OF S. FOSCA, TORCELLO.

STEEPLE OF S. STEPHEN'S CATHEDRAL, VIENNA,
AUSTRIA.

a   *b*

STILTED ARCHES IN VENICE; *a.* CALLE DEL PISTOR; *b.*
SALIZZADA S. LIO.

STONE CUTTING, FIG. 2: DETAIL OF A TEMPLE AT
THEBES.

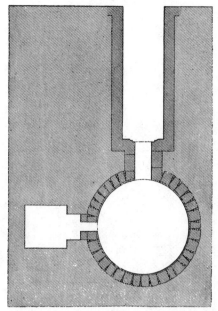

STONE CUTTING, FIG. 3: THAT OF THE PRE-HEL-
LENIC EPOCH. A THOLOS AT MYCENÆ; A VERY
LARGE TOMBAL CHAMBER, WITH DROMOS, ALL
FACED WITH STONE.

STONE CUTTING, FIG. 6: BARREL VAULT OF PECULIAR CONSTRUCTION; NYMPHÆUM AT NÎMES, SOUTH
OF FRANCE; ROMAN IMPERIAL WORK.

STONE CUTTING, FIG. 7: DETAIL OF NYMPHÆUM,
NÎMES. SEE CUT ABOVE.

STONE CUTTING, FIG. 8: FRENCH GOTHIC WORK OF THE BEST
PERIOD; CHURCH OF S. EUSÈBE, AUXERRE: 13TH CENTURY.

STONE CUTTING, FIG. 9: FINELY FINISHED WORK OF THE FRENCH RENAISSANCE

STONEHENGE, NEAR SALISBURY, WILTSHIRE, ENGLAND.

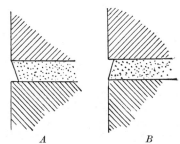

A   B

STRIKE: STRUCK JOINTS IN BRICK OR STONE
FACING. *A* IS EASY TO MAKE BUT LEAVES
A SHOULDER TO HOLD WATER. *B* SHEDS
WATER WELL, THE MORTAR PROTECTS THE
BRICK BELOW AND IS ALSO LESS VISIBLE, SO
THAT THE WALL REMAINS OF A MORE UNI-
FORM COLOUR.

SWITZERLAND, ARCHITECTURE OF: TOWN HALL OF
ZURICH; C. 1700.

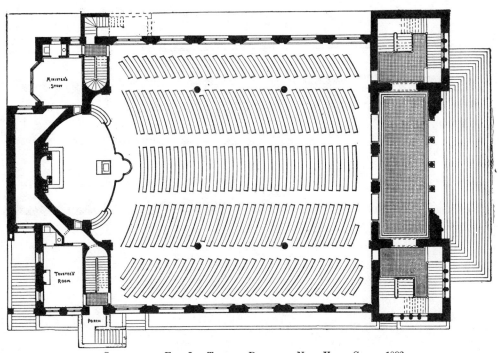

SYNAGOGUE, FIG. I.: TEMPLE BETH-EL, NEW YORK CITY; 1892.

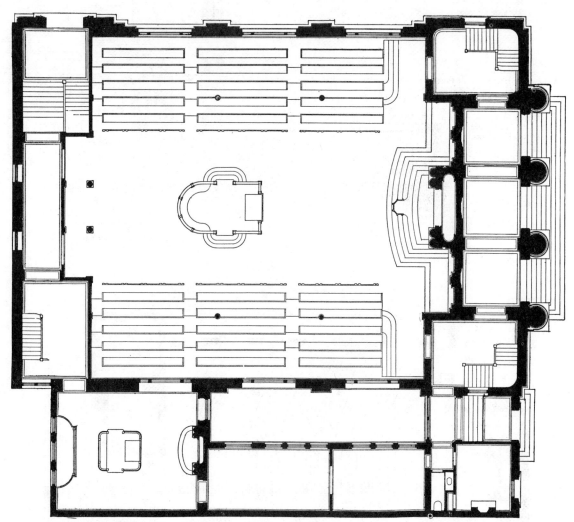

SYNAGOGUE, FIG. II.: WEST SEVENTIETH STREET, NEW YORK. AS THE ARK MUST BE AT THE EAST END, IT IS SET AGAINST THE INNER WALL OF THE GREAT VESTIBULE, FROM WHICH THE GROUND STORY IS ENTERED AT RIGHT AND LEFT.

SYRIA, ARCHITECTURE OF: THE SO-CALLED PRETORIUM AT MUSMIGEH, BUILT ABOUT 170 A.D.

TEMPLE AT BAALBEC; 2ND CENTURY.

DETAILS OF THE CHURCH OF S. SIMEON STYLITES AT KALAT SEMÁN.

DOOR OF A TOMB IN SYRIA.

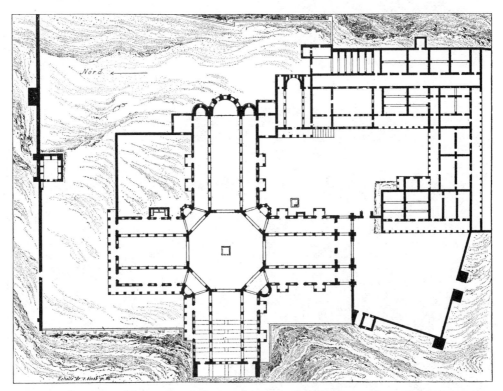

CHURCH AND CONVENT OF S. SIMEON STYLITES: 6TH CENTURY. KALAT SEMÁN.

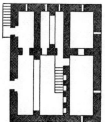

PLAN OF THE STONE HOUSE AT DOUMA: 2ND–3RD
CENTURY.

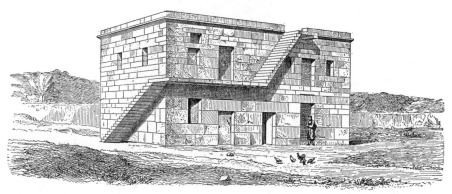

STONE HOUSE AT CHAQQA: 2ND–3RD CENTURY.

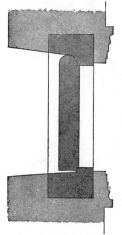

PLAN OF DOOR OF A TOMB IN SYRIA.

TABERNACLE: HADDISCOL CHURCH, NORFOLK-
SHIRE; ABOUT 1160.

STONE DOOR IN THE BASILICA OF TAFKHA.

TABERNACLE: LADY CHAPEL, EXETER CATHE-
DRAL; c. 1280.

From this and the Kiddington example figures have been removed.

TABERNACLE: QUEEN ELEANOR'S CROSS AT
NORTHAMPTON; 1294.

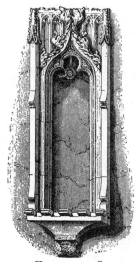

TABERNACLE: KIDDINGTON CHURCH, OXFORD-
SHIRE; c. 1450.

TABLET IN THE VON DER LINDE HOUSE; STOCK-
HOLM, SWEDEN.

TEMPLE, FIG. 1: THAT OF KHUNSU, BUILT BY RAMSES III. AT KARNAK; THE HYPÆTHRAL COURT.

TEMPLE, FIG. 2: THAT OF NEPTUNE AT PÆSTUM; SECTION SHOWING TWO STORIED C DIVIDING NAOS.

TEMPLE, FIG. 3: THAT OF NEPTUNE AT PÆSTUM; SEE THE SECTION, FIG. 2.

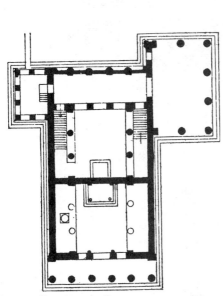

TEMPLE, FIG. 4: THE ERECHTHEUM AT ATHENS; CONTAINING AT LEAST THREE SEPARATE SHRINES. HEXASTYLE IONIC PORTICO PARTLY INDICATED BY THE THREE PORTICOES; TETRASTYLE IONIC PORTICO WITH TWO COLUMNS IN RETURN; AND BELOW, TETRASTYLE PORTICO OF CARYATIDES WITH TWO FIGURES IN RETURN.

TEMPLE, FIG. 5: THAT OF VESTA AT TIVOLI; RESTORATION OF J. A. LEVEIL.

TEMPLE, FIG. 7: THAT AT ELLORA, INDIA.

TEMPLE OF THE WINDS, AT ATHENS.

343

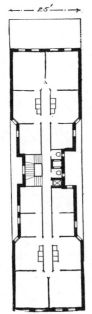

TENEMENT HOUSE, FIG. 1. PLAN WITH FOUR TENEMENTS IN A STORY. SITTING ROOMS AT FRONT AND REAR.

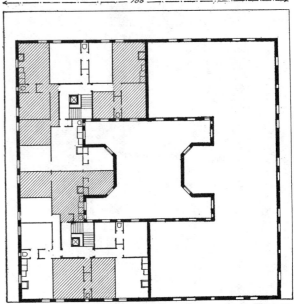

TENEMENT HOUSE ON A PLOT 100 FEET SQUARE, WITH NARROW OUTER RESERVATIONS FOR LIGHT AND AIR, AND A CENTRAL COURT; SIXTEEN TENEMENTS IN EACH STORY. FIG. 2.

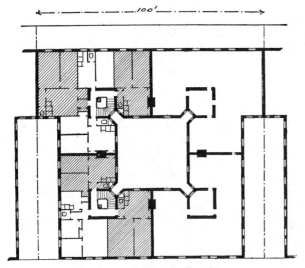

TENEMENT HOUSE, FIG. 3.

A model plan approved by reform committees in New York, 1900. It is adapted to plots 100 feet square, each plot containing fourteen tenements, and the deep and narrow courts (about 20 by 60 feet) are open in every case to the street, while a reserved space 10 feet wide is left between the rear wall and the centre line of the block.

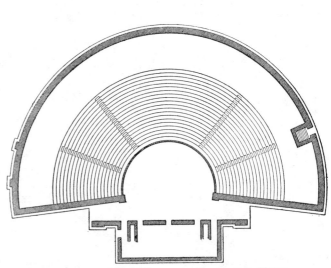

THEATRE OF ROMAN STYLE AT IASSUS, ASIA MINOR.

THEATRE: RUINS OF THE LARGER ONE AT POMPEII.

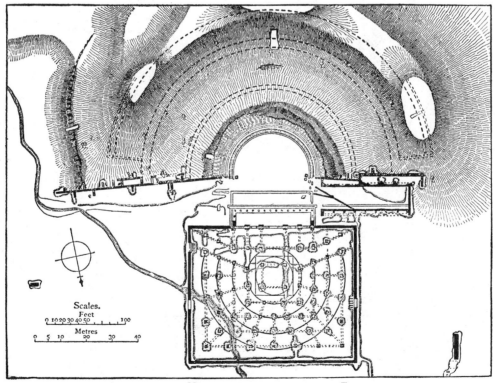

THERSILIUM AT MEGALOPOLIS; WITH ADJOINING THEATRE.

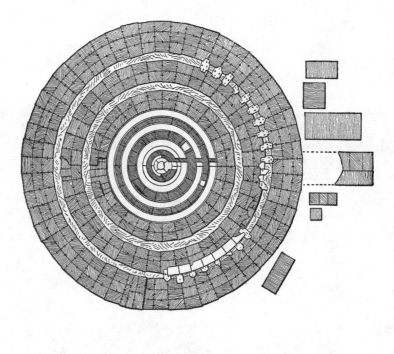

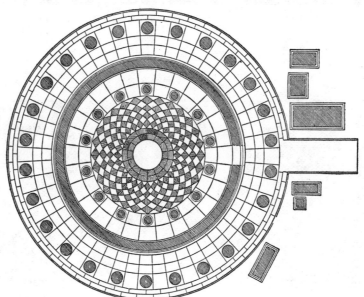

THOLOS AT EPIDAURUS AS IT EXISTS, AND AS RESTORED. THE OUTER ORDER
IS DORIC; THAT WITHIN CORINTHIAN.

  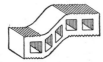

TILES OF BAKED CLAY FOR HOLDING TOGETHER THE PARTS OF A HOLLOW WALL;
THE SLOPE COMING IN THE AIR SPACE.

TIPI OF BUFFALO HIDE;
DAKOTA TYPE.

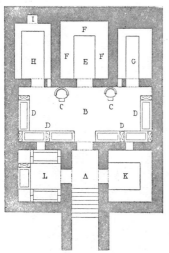

TOMB, FIG. 1, OF THE TWO SEATS, CERVETRI,
ITALY; PLAN.

A, entrance. B, outer chamber with the two seats, C, and
later sarcophagi, D. E, G, H, K, Tombal chambers with
platforms, F, on which bodies were laid. L, chamber with
sarcophagi.

TOMB, FIG. 2, OF THE TWO SEATS, AT CERVETRI, ITALY. SEE PLAN.

TOMB, FIG. 3, THAT OF CAECILIA METELLA, NEAR ROME, 1ST CENTURY, B.C.   THE BATTLEMENTS ARE
MEDIÆVAL, THE TOWER HAVING BEEN INCLUDED IN A CASTLE. SEE FIG. 4

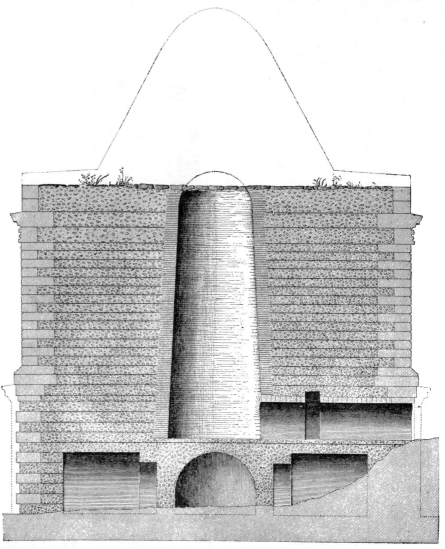

TOMB, FIG. 4, SECTION (SEE FIG. 3). THE SOLID CORE OF MASONRY FACED WITH BLOCKS OF CUT
STONE WAS ORIGINALLY CROWNED BY A CONICAL OR STEPPED ROOF-LIKE COVERING.

TOMB, FIG. 5, THAT OF IAMLICHUS, PALMYRA, A.D. 83.

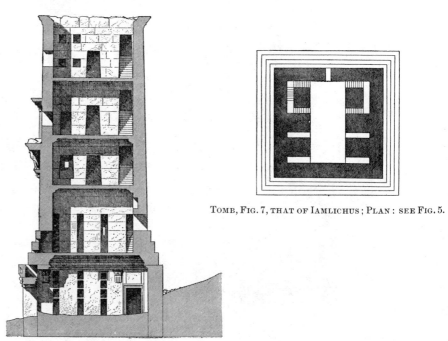

TOMB, FIG. 6, THAT OF IAMLICHUS; SECTION,
SEE FIG. 5.

TOMB, FIG. 7, THAT OF IAMLICHUS; PLAN: SEE FIG. 5.

348

TOMB, FIG. 8, 4TH CENTURY A.D., AT DANA, IN SYRIA.

TOMB, FIG. 9, 4TH CENTURY A.D.; ABOUT 35 FEET SQUARE; KHURBET-HÂSS, IN SYRIA.

TOMB, FIG. 11, SURROUNDING A COURT OR CHURCHYARD AT MESCHUM, SYRIA.

TOMB, FIG. 10, THOSE AT KHURBET-HÂSS, IN SYRIA; SEE FIG. 9.

TOMB, FIG. 17, IN CLOISTER S. ANTONIO, PADUA; A MURAL PAINTING UNDER THE CANOPY.

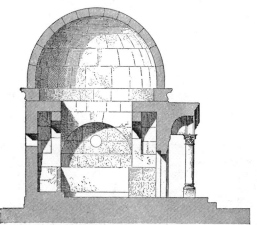

TOMB, FIG. 12, OF 6TH CENTURY, AT ROUEIHA, SYRIA; SEVENTEEN FEET SQUARE WITHOUT THE LITTLE PORCH. THIS FORM, WITH CUPOLA, HAS BEEN COPIED BY THE MOSLEM PEOPLES FOR CENTURIES.

TOMB, FIG. 19, IN THE PAVEMENT, CHURCH OF S. M. DEL POPOLO, ROME, 1479.

TOMB, FIG. 16, THAT OF MASTINO II DELLA SCALA; C. 1351, A.D., AT VERONA.

Tomb, Fig. 13, that of Bishop Giles of Bridport, 1262, a.d. Cathedral at Salisbury, Wiltshire. Altar Tomb under Canopy.

TOMB, FIG. 14, OF 14TH CENTURY, ASSISI, IN UMBRIA; CHURCH OF S. FRANCESCO.

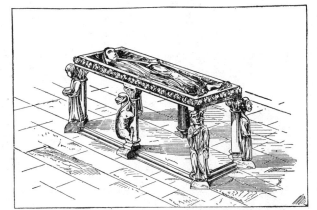

TOMB, FIG. 15, IN A CHURCH AT LIMBURG, GERMANY; 14TH CENTURY.

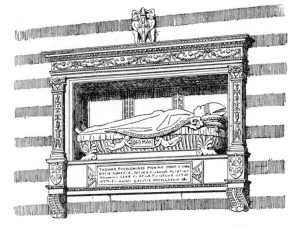

TOMB, FIG. 20, SIENA CATHEDRAL, C. 1483.

TOMB, FIG. 21, THAT OF THE SONS OF CHARLES VIII., AT TOURS.

TOMB, FIG. 22, THAT OF BENEDETTO PESARO, CHURCH OF
S. MARIA GLORIOSA DEI FRARI, VENICE.

354

TORCH HOLDER; BRONZE, 15TH CENTURY; PALAZZO
DEL MAGNIFICO, SIENA.

TORCH HOLDER; BRONZE, 15TH CENTURY; PALAZZO
DEL MAGNIFICO, SIENA.

TOWER; CENTRAL TOWER OF CHURCH AT NOGENT
LES VIERGES (OISE), FRANCE, 12TH CENTURY.

TOWER; GROUP OF FIVE TOWERS; 10TH AND 11TH CENTURIES;
TOURNAI, BELGIUM.

TOWER; RAVENSTHORPE, NORTHAMPTONSHIRE;
C. 1300.

TOWER; BRISLINGTON, SOMERSETSHIRE; C. 1500.

TOWER OF TOWN CHURCH, BOZEN, TYROL; C. 1590.

TOWER; TOWN CHURCH OF GRAZ, IN AUSTRIA;
C. 1780.

TOWER; CATHEDRAL OF LAON; NORTHWEST TOWER.

TOWER; CHURCH OF S. ANNA AT VIENNA; C. 1747.

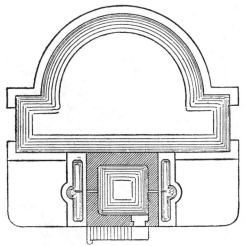

WATER TOWER FOR A FARM; PLAN, SHOWING
TWO CATTLE TROUGHS AND LARGE BASIN FOR
FILLING VESSELS. THE TOWER ITSELF IS A
RESERVOIR.

WATER TOWER; SEE THE PLAN.

TRABEATED CONSTRUCTION; CLOISTER OF S. M. DELLA PACE, ROME; UPPER STORY. ONE OF THE
EARLIEST WORKS OF BRAMANTE; C. 1495.

TRACERY, FIG. 1; S. MARTIN DES CHAMPS, PARIS;
C. 1220.

TRACERY, FIG. 2; CHARTRES CATHEDRAL; C. 1220.

TRACERY, FIG. 3; ROUEN CATHEDRAL, UPPER
SACRISTY; EXEMPLIFYING A TRANSITION FROM
PLATE TO BAR TRACERY, THOUGH OF A LATE
EPOCH.

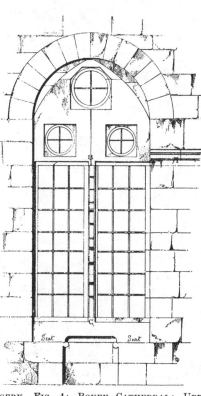

TRACERY, FIG. 4; ROUEN CATHEDRAL; UPPER
SACRISTY; INTERIOR ELEVATION.

TRACERY, FIG. 5; S. ANDREA, MANTUA. EXAMPLE
OF PLATE TRACERY WORKED IN BRICK.

358

TRACERY, FIG. 7: TOMB IN THE ABBEY OF LAACK,
RHENISH PRUSSIA.

TRACERY, FIG. 6; CATHEDRAL OF TOUL (FRANCE); CLOISTER.

TRACERY, FIG. 8; ARCADE OF THE DUCAL PALACE, VENICE.

TRACERY, FIG. 9; CARLISLE CATHEDRAL, NORTHUMBERLAND;
c. 1300, A.D.

TRACERY, FIG. 10; CHURCH OF FRIARY, READING,
ENGLAND, A.D. 1306.

TRACERY, FIG. 11; KINGSTHORPE, NORTHAMPTON-
SHIRE, C. 1350.

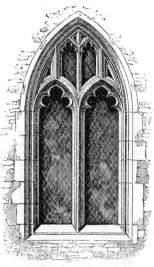

TRACERY, FIG. 12; MINSTER LOVEL, OXFORDSHIRE;
c. 1430.

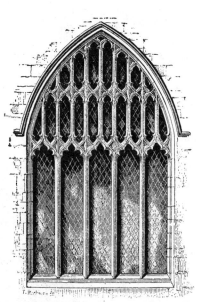

TRACERY, FIG. 13; SWINBROOK, OXON; c. 1500.

360

TRACERY, FIG. 14; PARAPET OF S. GERVAIS, FALAISE, IN NORMANDY.

TRACERY, FIG. 15; PARAPET OF S. GERVAIS, FALAISE, IN NORMANDY.

TRACERY, FIG. 16; RUSHDEN CHURCH, NORTHAMPTONSHIRE; C. 1450.

TRACERY, FIG. 17; RUSHDEN CHURCH, NORTHAMPTONSHIRE; C. 1450.

TRACERY, FIG. 18; WINDOW TRACERY, RICHLY ADORNED, ENGLISH; ABOUT 1400.

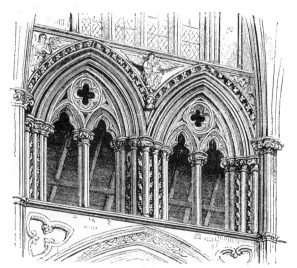

TRIFORIUM; LINCOLN CATHEDRAL, C. 1260.

TRILITH AT ST. NAZAIRE (LOIRE-INFÉRIEURE), FRANCE.

TUMULUS, ILE DE GAVR'INIS (MORBIHAN), FRANCE; SECTION SHOW-
ING LONG CISTVAEN, THE SLABS INCISED WITH PATTERNS.

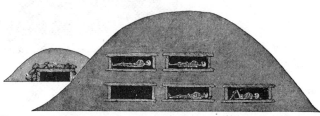

TUMULUS IN THE ORKNEY ISLANDS, SECTION SHOWING SEPARATE
CHAMBERS FOR BURIAL MADE OF FLAT STONES.

TURRET; GLASTONBURY ABBEY, C. 1200; IT COVERS
THE HEAD OF A WINDING STAIR AND GIVES
ACCESS TO THE ROOFS.

TURRET; S. MARY'S, BEVERLY; C. 1450.

TURRET; TOWER WITH STAIRCASE TURRET;
GORING, OXFORDSHIRE; C. 1120.

TYMPANUM OF A WINDOW IN EL-BARAH, SYRIA;
5TH TO 6TH CENTURY.

UNITED STATES: HOUSE AT PORTSMOUTH, N. H.

UNITED STATES: HOUSE AT PIGEON COVE, MASS., 1643.

UNITED STATES: FARMHOUSE NEAR HINGHAM, MASS.

UNITED STATES: ROGER WILLIAMS HOUSE, SALEM, MASS., 1635.

363

UNITED STATES: CHURCH AT HINGHAM, MASS., 1681.

UNITED STATES: THE ROYALL MANSION, MEDFORD, MASS.

United States: House on Long Island.

United States: Old State House, Boston, 1748.

United States: Van Rensselaer House, Greenbush, N.Y.

United States: Vassall Mansion (since 1837 Longfellow's House), Cambridge, Mass., 1759.

United States: Apthorpe House, New York, N.Y.

UNITED STATES: CHURCH AT RICHMOND, VA., 1811.

UNITED STATES: UNIVERSITY OF VIRGINIA,
CHARLOTTESVILLE, VA., 1817.

UNITED STATES: OLD NORTH CHURCH, NEW
HAVEN, CONN.

UNITED STATES: LIBRARY, BOSTON, MASS.

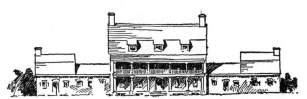

UNITED STATES: HOUSE IN MARYLAND; TYPICAL MANSION
WITH OUTHOUSES; 18TH CENTURY.

UNITED STATES: FIRST CHURCH, NEW
HAVEN, CONN.

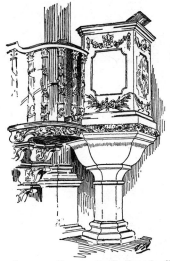

UNITED STATES: PULPIT IN S. PAUL'S CHAPEL,
NEW YORK; CHURCH BUILT 1764–1766.

UNITED STATES: DWIGHT HOUSE, SPRINGFIELD, MASS., 1764.

UNITED STATES: MORRIS HOUSE, NEW YORK, N. Y., 1762.

VANE FROM
STOCKHOLM,
SWEDEN.

VASE, MARBLE; AT CHÂTEAU OF FONTAINEBLEAU,
FRANCE.

VASE, MARBLE; ANCIENT ROMAN WORK IN THE
MUSEUM OF THE VATICAN, ROME.

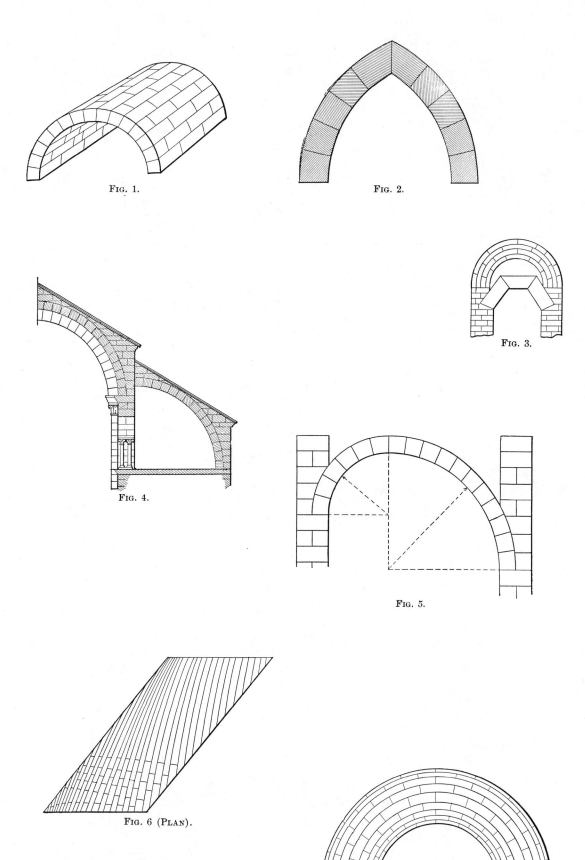

Fig. 1.

Fig. 2.

Fig. 3.

Fig. 4.

Fig. 5.

Fig. 6 (Plan).

Fig. 7 (Plan).

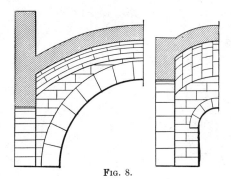

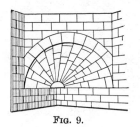

F<small>IG</small>. 8.

F<small>IG</small>. 9.

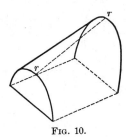

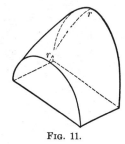

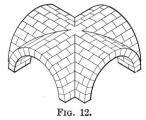

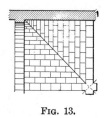

F<small>IG</small>. 10.

F<small>IG</small>. 11.

F<small>IG</small>. 12.

F<small>IG</small>. 13.

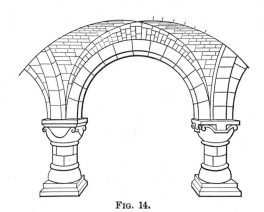

F<small>IG</small>. 14.

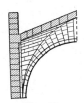

F<small>IG</small>. 15.

F<small>IG</small>. 16.

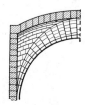

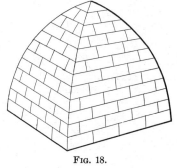

F<small>IG</small>. 17.

F<small>IG</small>. 18.

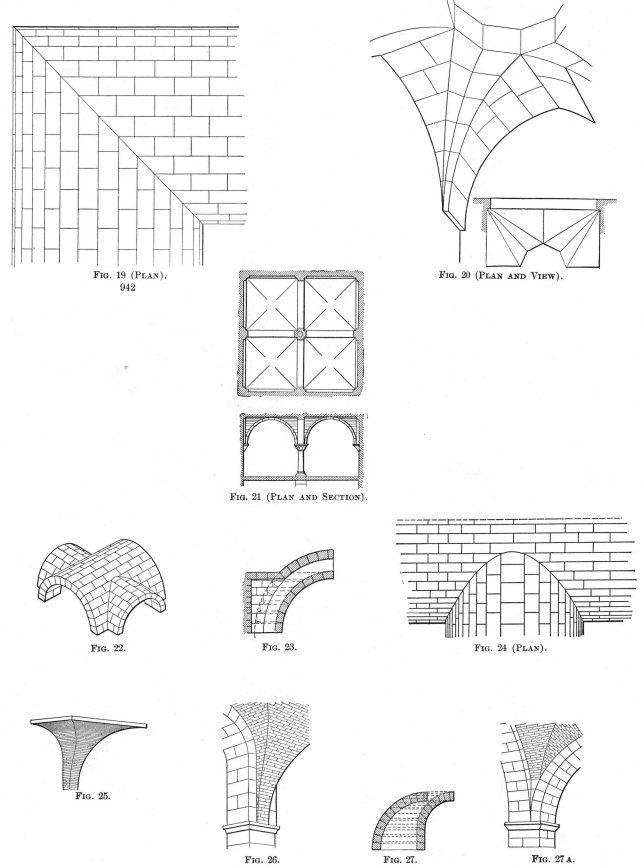

FIG. 19 (PLAN).
942

FIG. 20 (PLAN AND VIEW).

FIG. 21 (PLAN AND SECTION).

FIG. 22.

FIG. 23.

FIG. 24 (PLAN).

FIG. 25.

FIG. 26.

FIG. 27.

FIG. 27 A.

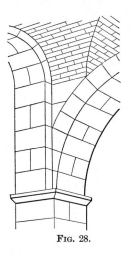

Fig. 28.

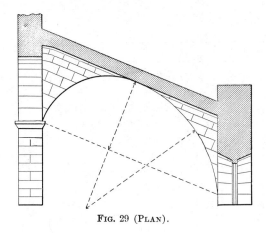

Fig. 29 (Plan).

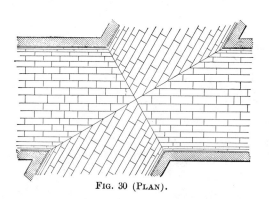

Fig. 30 (Plan).

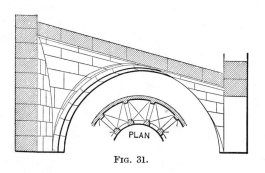

PLAN

Fig. 31.

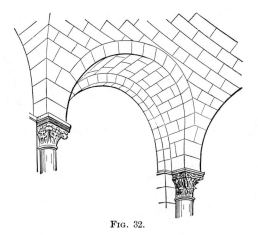

Fig. 32.

Fig. 33.

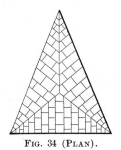

Fig. 34 (Plan).

Fig. 35 (Plan).

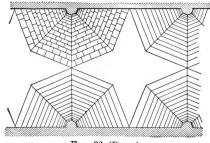

Fig. 36 (Plan).

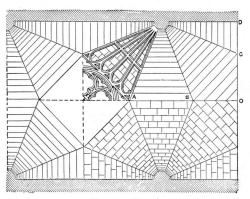

Fig. 37 (Plan).

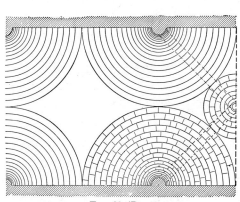

Fig. 38 (Plan).

Fig. 39 (Plan).

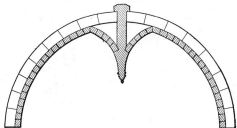

Fig. 40.

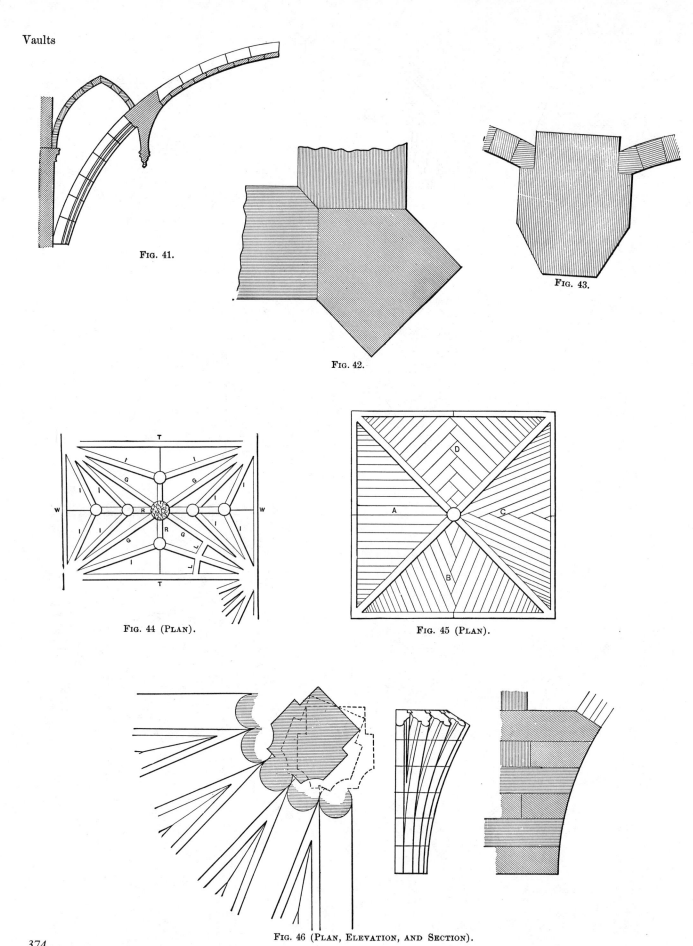

FIG. 41.

FIG. 42.

FIG. 43.

FIG. 44 (PLAN).

FIG. 45 (PLAN).

FIG. 46 (PLAN, ELEVATION, AND SECTION).

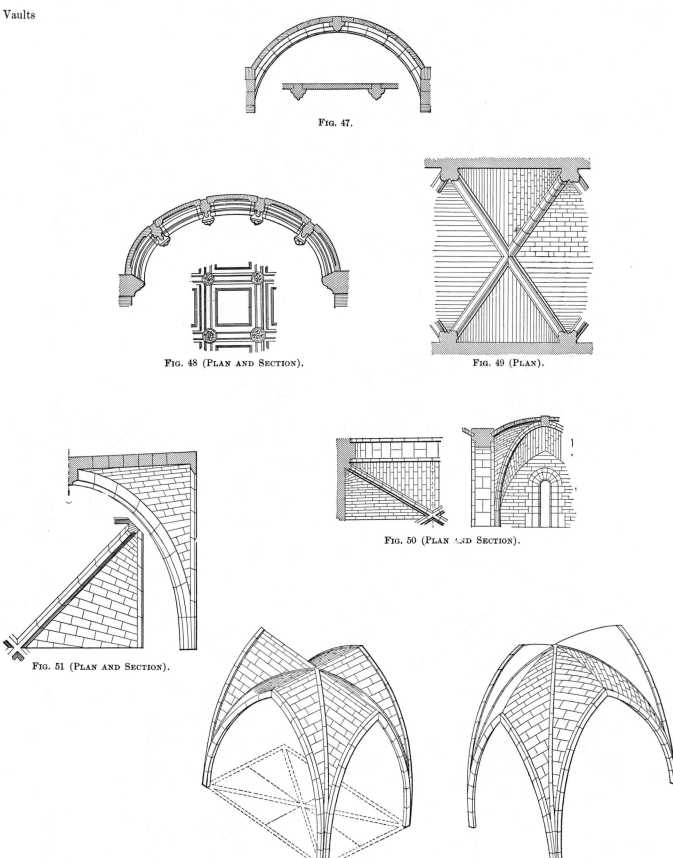

FIG. 47.

FIG. 48 (PLAN AND SECTION).

FIG. 49 (PLAN).

FIG. 50 (PLAN AND SECTION).

FIG. 51 (PLAN AND SECTION).

FIG. 52.

FIG. 53.

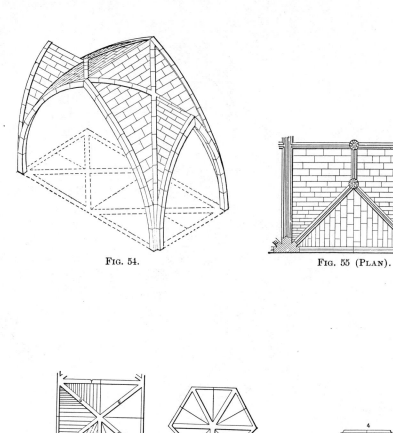

Fig. 54.

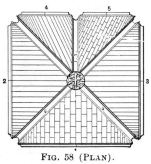

Fig. 55 (Plan).

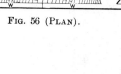

Fig. 56 (Plan).

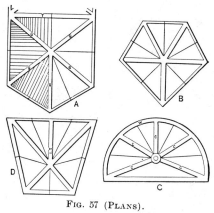

Fig. 57 (Plans).

Fig. 58 (Plan).

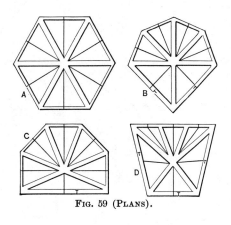

Fig. 59 (Plans).

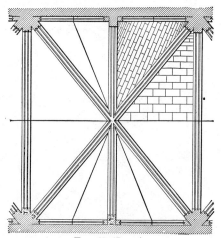

Fig. 60 (Plan).

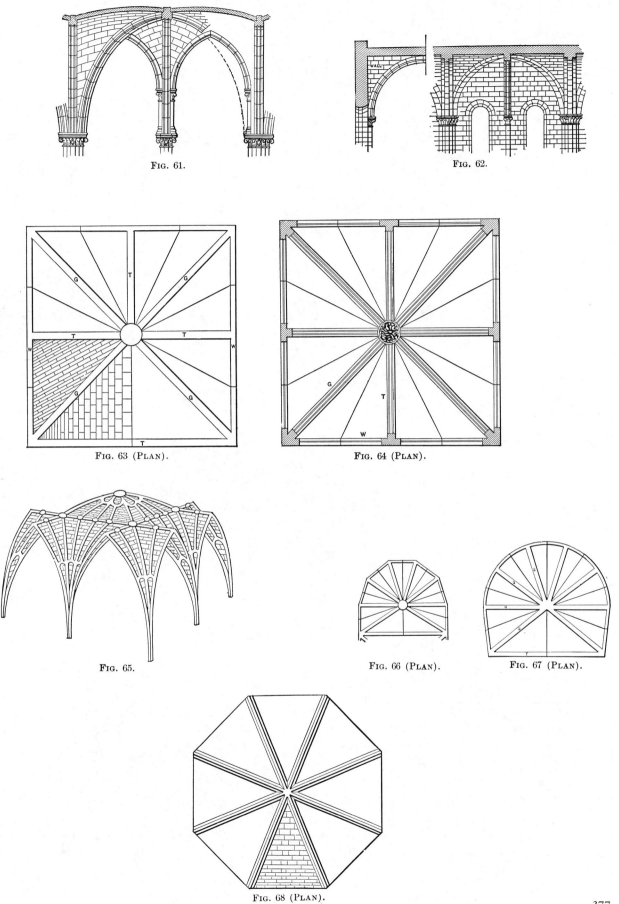

FIG. 61.

FIG. 62.

FIG. 63 (PLAN).

FIG. 64 (PLAN).

FIG. 65.

FIG. 66 (PLAN).

FIG. 67 (PLAN).

FIG. 68 (PLAN).

Vaults

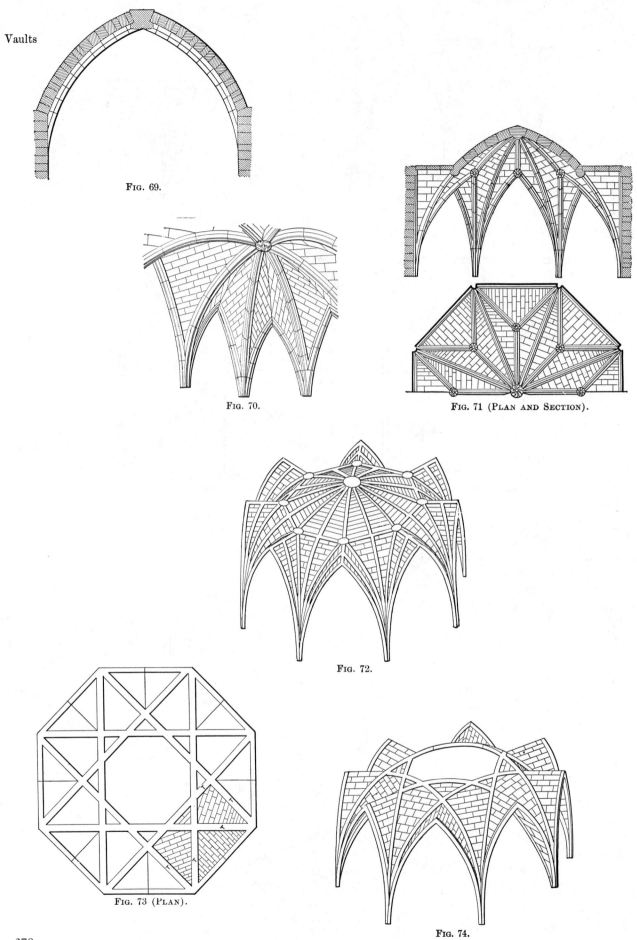

Fig. 69.

Fig. 70.

Fig. 71 (Plan and Section).

Fig. 72.

Fig. 73 (Plan).

Fig. 74.

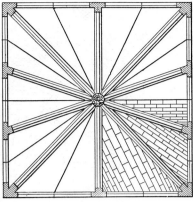

FIG. 75 (PLAN).

FIG. 76 (PLAN).

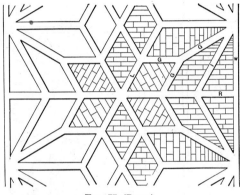

FIG. 77 (PLAN).

FIG. 78 (PLAN).

FIG. 79 (PLAN).

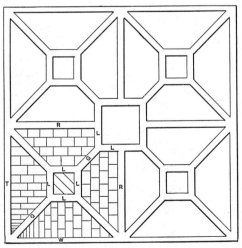

FIG. 80 (PLAN).

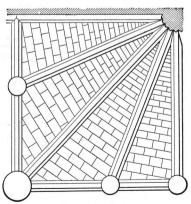

FIG. 81 (PLAN).

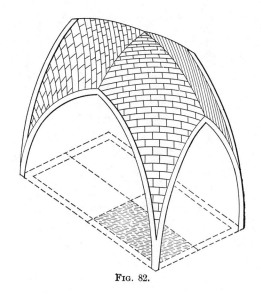

FIG. 82.

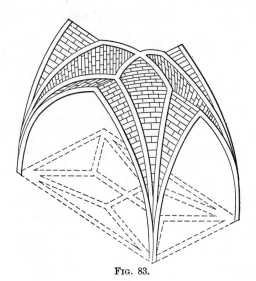

FIG. 83.

FIG. 84 (PLAN).

FIG. 85 (PLAN).

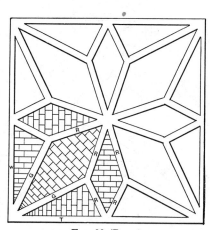

FIG. 86 (PLAN).

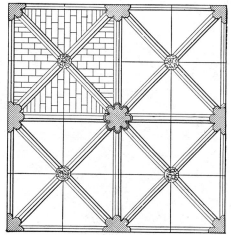

FIG. 87 (PLAN).

FIG. 88 (SEE FIG. 87).

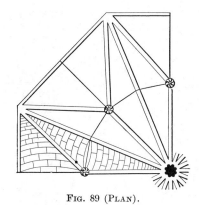

FIG. 89 (PLAN).

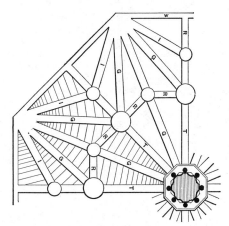

FIG. 90 (PLAN).

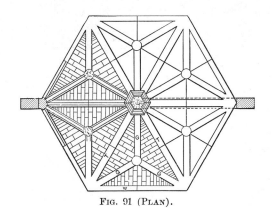

FIG. 91 (PLAN).

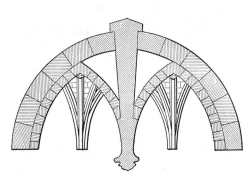

FIG. 92 (SECTION, SEE FIG. 91).

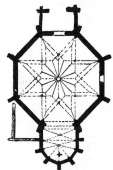

VAULTING OF THE KARLSHOFER CHURCH, PRAGUE,
BOHEMIA; ALL SPRINGING FROM THE ANGLES
OF THE OUTER OCTAGON, MAKING WHAT IS
CALLED A GOTHIC DOME.

FAN VAULTING; CLOISTERS GLOUCESTER CATHEDRAL, C. 1450.

VAULTING, NEOCLASSIC; CHURCH OF S. PETER, ROME; INTERIOR.

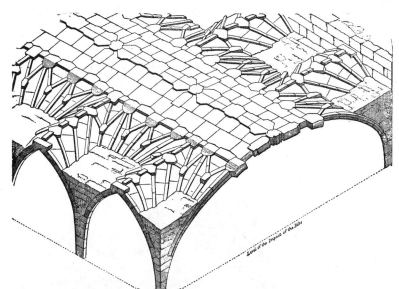

FAN VAULTING; CONSTRUCTION OF CHOIR ROOF, S. GEORGE'S CHAPEL, WINDSOR CASTLE. THE MIDDLE SECTION IS NOT RIBBED AT ALL BUT VAULTED IN SOLID BLOCKS. THE HAUNCHES ARE KEPT IN PLACE BY FILLING OF ROUGH MASONRY.

VAULTING SHAFT; MÜNSTERMAIFELD, RHENISH PRUSSIA. THE SHAFTS PROPER SPRING FROM CULS-DE-LAMPE AND ARE ONLY TWO FEET LONG.

VAULTING SHAFT; THE NEAR ANGLE, BETWEEN CHOIR AND TRANSEPT, HAS A SHAFT FOR EACH GREAT GROUP OF RIBS, FIVE IN ALL.

WARM
FRESH AIR

COLD
FRESH AIR

b

RADIATOR

b

VENTILATION; FIG. 1.

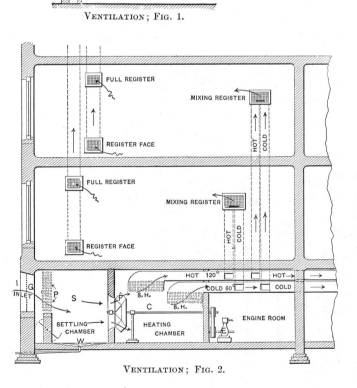

FULL REGISTER

MIXING REGISTER

REGISTER FACE

HOT COLD

FULL REGISTER

MIXING REGISTER

REGISTER FACE

HOT COLD

INLET

G

P S

P

S. H.

C

S. H.

HOT 120°

COLD 60

HOT

COLD

SETTLING CHAMBER

W

HEATING CHAMBER

ENGINE ROOM

VENTILATION; FIG. 2.

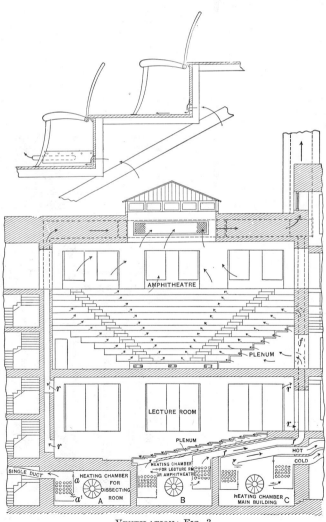

AMPHITHEATRE

PLENUM

r

r

LECTURE ROOM

PLENUM

r

r

f

f

HOT
COLD

SINGLE DUCT

a

a

HEATING CHAMBER FOR DISSECTING ROOM

A

HEATING CHAMBER FOR LECTURE RM OR AMPHITHEATRE

B

HEATING CHAMBER MAIN BUILDING

C

VENTILATION; FIG. 3.

VESTIBULE OF A HOUSE NEAR THE CHURCH S. M. DELLA PACE, ROME.

VERA DA POZZO OF BRONZE, IN COURT OF DUCAL PALACE, VENICE.

VESTIBULE IN PALAZZO MACCARANI, ROME.

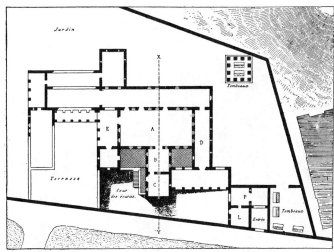

A. Great hall, with one or two stories over.

B, C. Lower buildings ; C is probably a kitchen.

D. Chief corridor of entrance.

E. Portico, where was probably the principal staircase.

L. Porter's lodge.

P. Entrance to the villa indirect, leading through three vestibules which could be closed.

VILLA, EL-BARAH, SYRIA; PLAN PARTLY RESTORED.

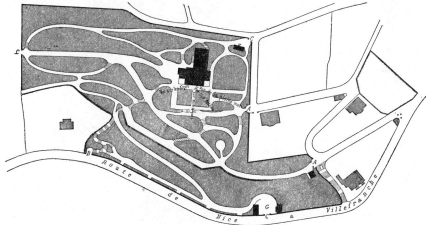

VILLA; AT MONTBORON, NEAR NICE (ALPES-MARITIMES), FRANCE.

A. Principal entrances; vehicles mounting by roads which pass beyond the house, and from which flights of steps ascend the hill.

B. Entrance for pedestrians by continuous path, partly a stair *a cordoni*.

C. Service entrances; that on the right below passing through the stable yard and thence by another wagon road to the level of that on the left which is on a level with the house.

D. Dwelling house.

E. Gardener's cottage.

F. Porter's lodge.

G. Stables and carriage house fronting on stable yard.

The unshaded parts are not included in the estate. The staircase *a cordoni* on the right above the word Villefranche is public, or at least common to several properties.

VILLA ROTONDA, NEAR VICENZA, 1560.

VOLUTE IN ROMANESQUE WORK; S. NICOLAS,
CAEN; C. 1100.

VOUSSOIR; CHURCH AT ARNSTEIN, RHENISH PRUS-
SIA. ARCH COMPOSED OF THREE VOUSSOIRS
AND TWO SKEW BACKS OR IMPOST BLOCKS,
EACH STONE CUT AWAY TO GIVE THE DECEP-
TIVE APPEARANCE OF A TRIPLE ARCH UNDER
AN ENCLOSING ARCH.

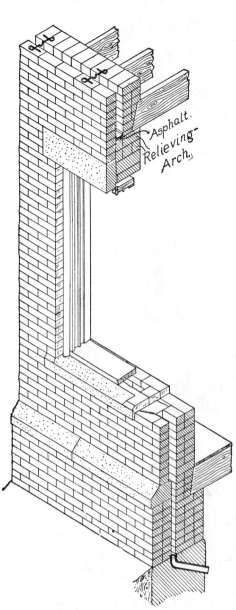

Asphalt.

Relieving-
Arch.

HOLLOW WALL; FIG. 1. THE MORE COMMON
FORM, USED FOR TWO-STORY AND THREE-
STORY BUILDINGS.

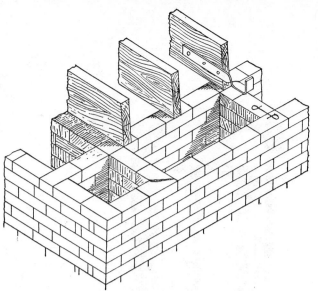

HOLLOW WALL, BUILT WITH LARGE CHAMBERS, A RARE FORM
BECAUSE MUCH GROUND SPACE IS USED.

WELL CURB, RATISBON CATHEDRAL, BAVARIA,
15TH CENTURY.

WICKYUP; PAI UTE FORM, OF TULE RUSHES; NEVADA. THERE IS GENERALLY AN OPENING AT TOP.

WELL CURB; PIAZZA DEI SIGNORI, VERONA. THE CURB PROPER AND THE COLUMNS AND CROSSBEAM ARE OF MARBLE; THE BOX WITH WICKET IS OF WOOD, AND TEMPORARY.

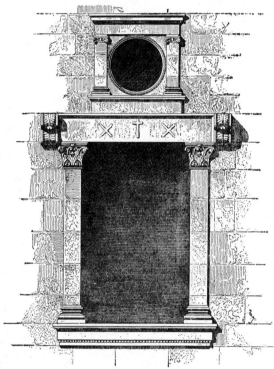

WINDOW, FIG. 1: IN THE PALACE AT CHAQQA OR SHAKKA; 3D CENTURY A.D.

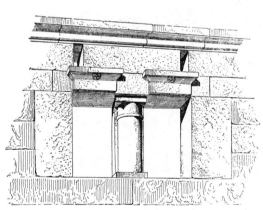

WINDOW, FIG. 2: PRIVATE HOUSE AT KHURBET-HASS.

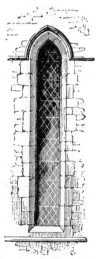

WINDOW, FIG. 3: WITNEY CHURCH, OXFORDSHIRE; c. 1220.

WINDOW, FIG. 4: CHURCH AT SAINT OUEN
(CALVADOS); C. 1225.

WINDOW, FIG. 5: WITNEY CHURCH, OXFORDSHIRE;

WINDOW, FIG. 6: SALISBURY CATHEDRAL; C. 1225.

WINDOW, FIG. 7: SALISBURY CATHEDRAL, NORTH TRANSEPT; C. 1225.

WINDOW, FIG. 8: STONE CHURCH, KENT; C. 1240.

389

WINDOW, FIG. 9: THE DEANERY, NORWICH; C. 1250.

WINDOW, FIG. 10: BOYTON CHURCH, WILTSHIRE; 1250.

WINDOW, FIG. 11: RUE BRICONNET, TOURS; C. 1260.

WINDOW, FIG. 12: THE BROLETTO, MONZA; C. 1270.

WINDOW, FIG. 13: HOUSE IN RUE DE RAPIN, TOURS; C. 1280.

WINDOW, FIG. 14: THURNING CHURCH, HUNTING-
DONSHIRE; C. 1300.

WINDOW, FIG. 15: THANINGTON CHURCH, KENT;
C. 1300.

WINDOW, FIG. 16: ARDLEY CHURCH, OXFORD-
SHIRE; C. 1350.

WINDOW, FIG. 17: DENFORD CHURCH, NORTH-
AMPTONSHIRE; C. 1350.

WINDOW, FIG. 18: APPLEFORD CHURCH, BERK-
SHIRE; C. 1350.

WINDOW, FIG. 19: SUTTON COURTENAY MANOR HOUSE, BERKSHIRE.

WINDOW, FIG. 20.

WINDOW, FIG. 21: WADSTENA, PROVINCE OF
OESTERGÖTLAND, SWEDEN.

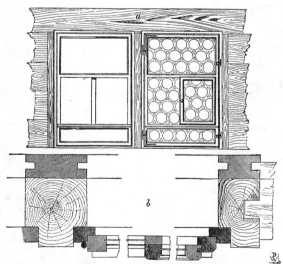

WINDOW, FIG. 22: DOUBLE, WITH WICKET, IN A SWISS
CHALET.

A, elevation ; *B*, plan at a scale four times as great; the clear width of
each half is about 2′ 8′′: the wicket about 1′ 2′′.

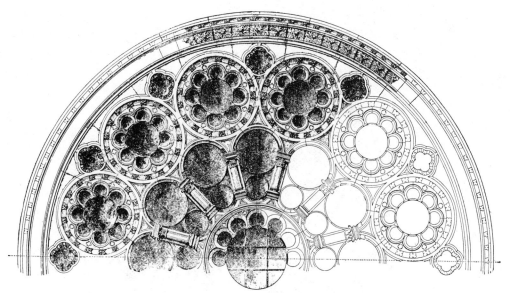

WINDOW, FIG. 23: ROSE WINDOW, CATHEDRAL OF CHARTRES, WEST FRONT, C. 1225.

WINDOW, FIG. 24: ROSE WINDOW, WEST FRONT OF CHURCH, MONTRÉAL (YONNE), BURGUNDY; C. 1250.

WINDOW, FIG. 25: ROSE WINDOW, BARFRESTON, KENT, C. 1180.

WINDOW, FIG. 26: ROSE WINDOW, BEVERLEY MINSTER, YORKSHIRE, C. 1220.

WINDOW, FIG. 27: ROSE WINDOW, BEAUVAIS CA-
THEDRAL; C. 1450.

WINDOW, FIG. 28: ROSE WINDOW, CATHEDRAL OF AUCH (GERS), FRANCE; C. 1250. THE SUBJECT OF
THE GLASS PAINTING (A GLORY OF ANGELS) IS INDICATED, BUT THE DRAWING IS NOT TRUSTWORTHY.

WINDOW SEAT IN ALNWICK CASTLE, NORTHUM-
BERLAND; C. 1310.

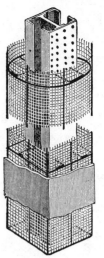

WIRE CLOTH USED
FOR LATHING, IN
FIREPROOF COVER-
ING OF A STEEL
COLUMN.

FIG. 1.

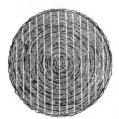

FIG. 2.

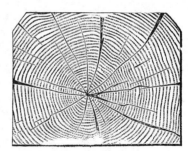

FIG. 2A: A PIECE OF HEWN TIMBER WHICH HAS
CHECKED IN DRYING.

FIG. 3.

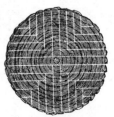

FIG. 3A: A METHOD OF SAWING BY WHICH WIDER
PLANKS OR BOARDS ARE GOT THAN IN FIG. 3
— BUT SLOW AND AWKWARD; USED FOR VERY
PRECIOUS WOOD.

WOOD, CONSTRUCTION IN, PART I., FIG. 1: INTERIOR HALL OF NURSTED COURT, KENT; 13TH CENTURY.

From the stone pillars there start uprights to support purlins, and diagonal braces which help support purlins and also carry transverse beams. From the centre of the transverse beams slender posts carry a plate upon which the collar beams rest. Except for the free use of diagonal braces this construction is very unscientific, but heavy timber and thick walls carry it through.

WOOD, CONSTRUCTION IN, PART I., FIG. 2; MAISON DU POIDS ROYAL; SAINT LÔ, FRANCE.

WOOD, CONSTRUCTION IN, PART I., FIG. 4.

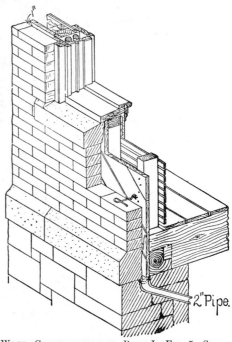

2"Pipe.

WOOD, CONSTRUCTION IN, PART I., FIG. 5. STRUC-
TURE OF A FRAME HOUSE FACED WITH FOUR
INCHES OF BRICKWORK AS DESCRIBED IN TEXT.

WREN, SIR CHRISTOPHER: STEEPLE OF S. MARY-
LE-BOW, 1677.